Alexis U. Floridi
Annette E. Stiefbold

THE UNCERTAIN ALLIANCE: THE CATHOLIC CHURCH AND LABOR IN LATIN AMERICA

MONOGRAPHS IN INTERNATIONAL AFFAIRS

CENTER FOR ADVANCED INTERNATIONAL STUDIES
UNIVERSITY OF MIAMI

ALEXIS U. FLORIDI, who was formerly on the staff of the Italian Catholic magazine *La Civiltà Cattolica,* and lecturer at Fordham University, has traveled widely in Latin America and is the author of several books, including *Radicalismo Católico Brasiliano*, written while he was a Senior Fellow at the Research Institute on Communist Affairs at Columbia University . . . .
ANNETTE E. STIEFBOLD, Research Associate at the Center for Advanced International Studies, formerly worked for the International Confederation of Free Trade Unions, contributed to *The Dilemmas of African Independence,* and is coauthor of *Convergence of Communism and Capitalism: The Soviet View.*

The
Lawrence Lee Pelletier
Library

Allegheny College

Library of Congress Catalog Number 73-92382
© University of Miami
Center for Advanced International Studies, 1973

PREFACE

This study is concerned with the entire range of Latin American Catholic workers' organizations, including those of agrarian workers; and with the increasing radicalization of some of the Catholic priests who serve them as advisers. The book is divided into two parts: first, a description and analysis of the multifaceted Church-labor relationship in Latin America; second, a documentary Appendix containing original source materials which illustrate major themes advanced by certain Church and labor spokesmen or organizations discussed in the text.

Within the text itself, Chapter One provides an initial general discussion of three basic trends in Latin American Catholicism and relates these to corresponding patterns of Church-labor relations. Chapters Two and Three are organized so as to highlight the apparent progression of individuals and movements characteristic of these patterns along a continuum from reform to radical. Chapter Four examines relevant findings of past studies of Latin American worker attitudes, and reviews some possible developmental trends in Church-State relations in the region.

Research for this study was undertaken originally by Alexis Floridi on the basis of a concept developed by the International Labor Program of Georgetown University and with initial financial support of that institution. Floridi's research involved two extended trips to Latin America, the first (1965-1967) spent in Brazil and Argentina, and the second (1971) in nine countries. Open-ended, unstructured interviews were conducted with Catholic clergymen and Catholic union officials representing a wide spectrum of political opinion. While the selection of respondents makes no claim to comprehensiveness or scientific randomization, it does reflect an illustrative cross-section of Catholic Church and labor views. This information was subsequently augmented by further research and analysis at the Center for Advanced International Studies of the University of Miami by Floridi and Annette Stiefbold, and in the Dominican Republic (1973) by Annette Stiefbold. Floridi wishes to acknowledge the generous support he received from Georgetown University, and particularly to thank Roy Godson for introducing him to key figures in the Latin American labor field. Stiefbold wishes to thank Kenneth Erickson, José Garcia Tatis, José Gómez Cerda, Daniel Montenegro, Manuel Ortega, Jaime Suchlicki, Elfriede Thiemann, and John Windmuller for their valuable assistance. None of these persons or institutions, however, bears responsibility for the materials or interpretations presented in the study.

ABBREVIATIONS AND ACRONYMS

AP	Popular Action (Brazil)
APRA	Popular American Revolutionary Alliance (Peru)
ASA	Antioquenan Syndical Association (Colombia)
ASICh	Chilean Syndical Action
ASICOL	Colombian Syndical Association
CASC	Autonomous Confederation of Christian Trade Unions (Dominican Republic)
CBTC	Brazilian Confederation of Christian Workers
CCT	Costa Rican Workers' Confederation
CELAM	Latin American Bishops' Council
CEP	Center for Studies and Publications (Lima, Peru)
CIDOC	Intercultural Documentation Center (Cuernavaca, Mexico)
CISC	International Confederation of Christian Trade Unions
CLASC	Latin American Confederation of Christian Trade Unions
CLAT	Latin American Workers' Central
CNBB	Brazilian National Bishops' Conference
CTM	Confederation of Mexican Workers
CTP	Peruvian Workers' Central
CUTCh	United Chilean Workers' Central
FANAL	National Federation of Farmers (Colombia)
FCL	Rural Latin American Federation
FORA	Argentinian Regional Workers' Federation
ICFTU	International Confederation of Free Trade Unions
ILADES	Latin American Institute for Doctrine and Social Studies (Chile)
JAC	Rural Catholic Youth (Brazil)
JOC	Catholic Working Youth (Brazil)
JUTRAM	Working Youth of Mexico
LADOC	Documentation Service, Division for Latin America, U.S. Catholic Conference
MEB	Movement for Basic Education (Brazil)
MPTW	Movement of Priests for the Third World (Argentina)
NADOC	Documentation Service, Lima, Peru
ONIS	National Office of Social Information (Peru)
ORIT	Interamerican Regional Organization of Workers
SETRAC	Selection of Catholic Workers (Colombia)
UCONAL	National Cooperatives Union (Colombia)
UTC	Colombian Workers' Union
WCL	World Confederation of Labor
WFTU	World Federation of Trade Unions

Contents

INTRODUCTION

The salience of Catholicism to the culture and history of Latin America has long been accepted as a primary characteristic of the region and a key factor in shaping its future. Today, as Turner observed in his recent book, *Catholicism and Political Development in Latin America*, "the Church is only one source of authority—both formal and informal—in Latin America, but it occupies a central position and the growing diversity of viewpoints within it makes its influences important subjects for study."[1]

The focus of the present study is the relationship between the Catholic Church and the Catholic-oriented labor movement in the contemporary climate of turmoil in Latin America. Both institutions are being rent by challenges to their established positions from both within and without. At the same time, they are seeking to redefine their own positions in an effort to maintain or re-establish their legitimacy and relevance in the volatile social, economic, and political context in which they exist. To assess these efforts it is necessary to ask what kinds of influence both the Church and labor wield and in what directions their influence is being channeled.

In discussing the Latin American labor movement one must be careful to distinguish, as Lodge does, between the traditional, generally urban, industrial and commercial trade unions and the mixed bag of peasant leagues, unions, or bands which are coming to play an increasingly important role in mobilizing the far more numerous rural inhabitants.[2] While membership figures are notoriously unreliable, perhaps 25 million Latin American workers are presently affiliated with conventional labor unions, but of these no more than 10 to 15 per cent are participating, dues-paying members in the North American sense.[3]

Latin American unions have the option of belonging to one of the three international labor confederations, or of remaining unaffiliated (see Table 1). The International Confederation of Free Trade Unions (ICFTU), to which the North American AFL-CIO belongs, has a Latin American regional affiliate, the Organización Regional Interamericana de Trabajo (ORIT). The Latin American regional affiliate of the Communist-influenced World Federation of Trade Unions (WFTU) has been the Confederación de Trabajadores de América Latina (CTAL), although there are plans to restructure the CTAL along neutralist lines. The international labor confederation of Chris-

---

[1] Frederick C. Turner, *Catholicism and Political Development in Latin America* (Chapel Hill: University of North Carolina Press, 1971), x.

[2] George C. Lodge, *Engines of Change* (New York: Alfred A. Knopf, 1970).

[3] *Ibid.*, p. 254. For a discussion of the problems involved in compiling Latin American labor statistics, see Tulo H. Montenegro, "Labor Statistics in Latin America," *Labor Developments Abroad,* U.S. Department of Labor, Bureau of Labor Statistics, October 1971.

Table I. Trade Union Members by International Trade Union Affiliations, 1964[1,2,3]

Country	Total Membership	%	ICFTU	%	WCL	%	WFTU	%	Without Interl. Affiliation	%
Central America										
Mexico	2,360,233	100.0	1,200,000	50.8	---	---	77,500	3.3	1,082,735[4]	45.9
Costa Rica	14,543	100.0	6,000	41.3	164	1.1	2,500	17.2	5,879	40.4
El Salvador	27,008	100.0	21,000	77.8	1,000	3.7	---	---	5,008	18.5
Guatemala	17,510	100.0	4,000	22.8	500	2.9	---	---	13,010	74.3
Honduras	27,102	100.0	21,365	78.8	625	2.3	---	---	5,112	18.9
Nicaragua	20,200	100.0	---	---	1,650	8.2	---	---	18,550	91.8
Panama	19,369	100.0	6,000	31.0	2,250	11.6	200	1.0	10,919	56.4
Caribbean										
Barbados	19,317	100.0	18,000	93.2	---	---	---	---	1,317	6.8
Cuba	1,510,075	100.0	9,250	0.6	---	---	---	---	1,500,825	99.4
Dominican Republic	67,875	100.0	60,000	88.4	6,300	9.3	---	---	1,575	2.3
Haiti	15,230	100.0	30	0.6	5,000	95.6	---	---	200	3.8
Jamaica	230,473	100.0	128,831	55.9	---	---	---	---	101,642	44.1
Trinidad & Tobago	71,152	100.0	69,202	97.3	---	---	1,950	2.7	---	---
South America										
Argentina	2,532,000	100.0	---	---	---	---	---	---	2,532,000	100.0
Bolivia	202,550	100.0	4,000	2.0	---	---	---	---	198,550	98.0
Brazil	2,053,788	100.0	1,950,000	94.9	---	---	---	---	103,788	5.1
Chile	556,108	100.0	97,000	17.4	20,000	3.6	99,000	17.8	340,108	61.2
Colombia	1,246,800	100.0	895,000	71.8	14,000	1.1	---	---	337,800	27.1
Ecuador	112,718	100.0	20,000	17.7	4,000	3.6	60,000	53.2	28,718	25.5
Guyana	75,561	100.0	46,000	60.9	---	---	---	---	29,561	39.1
Paraguay	54,000	100.0	(³)		---	---	4,000	7.4	50,000	92.6
Peru	605,050	100.0	500,000	82.6	30,000	4.9	---	---	75,050	12.4
Uruguay	191,916	100.0	15,000	7.8	2,000	1.0	11,000	5.7	163,916	85.4
Venezuela	1,590,429	100.0	1,300,000	81.7	20,000	1.3	240,000	15.1	30,429	1.9

Source: *Statistical Abstract of Latin America 1970*, UCLA Latin American Center, December 1971, adapted from the U.S. Department of Labor, *Directory of Hemisphere Labor Organizations: Western Hemisphere*, Vol. 1, May 1964.

[1]ICFTU—International Confederation of Free Trade Unions; WCL—World Confederation of Labor, formerly CISC—Confédération Internationale de Syndicats Chrétiens; WFTU—World Federation of Trade Unions.

[2]Most recent membership data were used. When there was reason to believe claimed membership figures were inflated and reliable estimates were available, estimated data were used. When membership figures were given as a range, the mean was used. Computation errors in the original table have been corrected.

[3]Complete membership data not available.

[4]Includes 135,000 nominal members of ATLAS [Peronist Agrupación de Trabajadores Latinoamericanos Sindicalistas].

tian orientation is the World Confederation of Labor (WCL, former Confédération Internationale de Sindicats Chrétiens—CISC). Its American regional affiliate is the Central Latinoamericana de Trabaja___ (CLAT, formerly the Confederación Latinoamericana de Sindicatos Cristianos—CLASC), whose headquarters were transferred in 1967 from Santiago, Chile, to Caracas, Venezuela. It is difficult to determine CLAT's total membership, particularly because of its large and fluctuating peasant component. In 1964 it claimed "influence over" 5,000,000 members, but this figure included sympathetic, but nonaffiliated, unions. Its actual membership is probably somewhat over one million, 60 per cent of which is peasant. Its strength is in the *Dominican Republic* (the Confederación Autónoma de Sindicatos Cristianos—CASC); *Ecuador* (the Confederación Ecuatoriana de Obreros Cristianos); *Venezuela* (the Confederación de Sindicatos Autónomos—CODESA; CLAT also has supporters within the dominant ORIT-affiliated Confederación de Trabajadores de Venezuela—CTV, and among the peasants of the Federación Campesina de Venezuela); and, to a lesser degree, *Colombia* (the Associación Sindical de Colombia—ASICOL, which faces strong opposition from the Church-supported Unión de Trabajadores de Colombia). The small CLAT affiliate in *Chile* is the Acción Sindical Chilena—ASICh.[4]

Historically, the objectives of Latin American labor unions have transcended limited economic demands. They have served a political function of national integration and a social function of easing the rural-to-urban transition of many workers. However, despite its intentions and articulated objectives, and its notable successes in such countries as Mexico and Venezuela, organized labor has come to be identified in the minds of many with the establishment. Supplanting it today as the cutting edge of worker radicalism in many cases are the newer, more heterogeneous peasant leagues. These organizations, encompassing perhaps 5 million people throughout Latin America, perform a wide variety of functions relevant to the problems of the peasant with respect to credit, marketing, land tenure, education, and housing.[5] The majority are "reformist-agrarian" in nature. They accept the legitimacy of the existing social order, but seek to reform those features that negatively

---

[4]See Michael J. Francis, "Revolutionary Labor in Latin America," *Journal of Inter-American Studies,* Vol. X, No. 4, October 1968, pp. 597-616, and U.S. Department of Labor, *Directory of the International Federation of Christian Trade Unions,* rev. ed., 1963.

[5]A Latin American authority has described as "one of the most important elements" characterizing the present process of change in Latin American societies "the tendency of peasants in some countries to differentiate themselves and organize and form politico-social movements to further their own interests"; see Aníbal Quijano Obregón, "Contemporary Peasant Movements," in Seymour Martin Lipset and Aldo Solari, eds., *Elites in Latin America* (New York: Oxford University Press, 1967), pp. 301ff.

affect the peasants' welfare. They are becoming increasingly militant, however, demanding more fundamental changes in the land-tenure system (i.e., in the social order itself), and resorting to illegal tactics such as land seizures. They are thus approaching the "revolutionary agrarian" type of peasant organization, which seeks, by direct action, to achieve the wholesale changes in the existing economic, social, and political system which it believes to be the *sine qua non* of genuine transformation of the countryside.[6]

Examples of all of these types of worker organizations will be discussed in the following chapters.

---

[6]Obregón also discusses the special case of the *Violencia* in Colombia, which he calls the unique Latin American example of the third type of peasant movement, "political banditry." Cf. Neale J. Pearson, who contrasts "genuine peasant unions . . . which protect the interest of their members against landowners, middle men and government agencies," such as the Confederación Campesina de Venezuela, with three other types: the personal political following (he includes the peasant leagues of Francisco Julião in northeast Brazil in this category), armed paramilitary groups, and producer cooperatives; in "Latin American Peasant Pressure Groups and the Modernization Process," *Journal of International Affairs,* Vol. XX, No. 2, 1968.

I
CRISIS IN CHURCH-LABOR RELATIONS

Today Latin America is undergoing profound economic, political, and social change. Regimes as diverse as the Peruvian military junta and the Mexican democratic government are seeking to alter existing structures in the hope of creating new institutions more responsive to the needs of modernizing and industrializing societies. New political forces generated by these processes are struggling to gain a greater voice in shaping the structures emerging from this transformation, and leaders of varying persuasions are contending for their loyalties. This process we shall call the Latin American revolution.[1]

Both the Catholic Church and the organized labor movement of Latin America are inexorably caught up in the Latin American revolution, and both have been rent by cleavages in attempting to respond to it and influence its direction.

There is no doubt that the social doctrine of the Catholic Church has evolved considerably in recent years. Yet, in some respects, it is this very evolution that now places the Church before its current dilemma: How far should the Church go in promoting social transformation in Latin America?

Within the Church there are three discernible trends. The first is reformist and gradualist. Pope Paul VI, the Council Vatican II, and most of the Latin American hierarchy subscribe to this "centrist-reformist" position, which seeks to correct the most flagrant abuses of the capitalist system, as it operates in Latin America, not to overthrow it. On labor matters, it is concerned chiefly with the professional upgrading of the workers and the strengthening of the trade union movement, but favors limiting the role of the Church itself to that of spiritual adviser. The second trend is "leftist-reformist." Its most prominent representative, Brazilian Archbishop Dom Helder Câmara, believing that capitalism is beyond reform, advocates socialism as the only means to put an end to Latin America's social and economic ills. Thirdly, there are some members of the extreme left, both laymen and priests, who regard violent revolution as the only realistic way to achieve the total structural transformation they demand. Camilo Torres, the Colombian guerrilla-priest, is the martyred hero of this group.

Many workers, for their part, distrust all three trends. Reformism promises too little change, while Marxist socialism, whether achieved by peaceful or violent means, they fear will result in the suppression of the trade union move-

---

[1] Robert J. Alexander, "The Latin American Labor Leader," in William H. Form and Albert A. Blum, eds., *Industrial Relations and Social Change* (Gainesville: University of Florida Press, 1965), pp. 70-86.

ment and the elimination of their own relatively privileged positions. Further-more, long accustomed to experiencing the influence of the Church in defend-ing the established order, many workers are suspicious of what they regard as continued Church paternalism in its attempts to channel and even lead their movement. Paradoxically, others berate the Church for its failure to provide stronger leadership. This stems from the Church's commitment, in an effort to overcome its former paternalistic image, to leave more decision-making flexibility to its followers, once the general guidelines of Church doc-trine have been enunciated. Thus, the fact that the Church no longer seeks to impose predetermined solutions to the continent's problems is regarded by many Latin Americans as intentional equivocation, in order to preserve its options with all regimes of the continent.

Summarizing in a few sentences such often amorphous and wide-ranging opinions as those sketched above necessarily leaves much unsaid. What we are dealing with are two complex and fragmented organizations, the Catholic Church in Latin America and the Catholic-oriented unions in the Latin Ameri-can labor movement. Moreover, words such as "structural transformation," "socialism," "revolution," and "violence" can reflect totally different conno-tations, depending on who is using them. The intention here has been to outline the broad parameters of the conflicts both within and between the Catholic Church and the labor movement. Subsequent illustrations will elaborate on these views.

The sense of frustration at what some workers regard as lack of attention by the Church to matters of vital concern to them came to a head at the time of the Second General Conference of Latin American Bishops (CELAM), held in Medellín, Colombia, in August-September, 1968.[2] The local Vatican nuncios decided against admitting any representatives from the Lat-in American Federation of Christian Trade Unions (CLASC) to the confer-ence as lay consultants, and the CLASC leadership reacted vehemently to this perceived insult. Writing as the representative of "five million workers and *campesinos*, men, women and youth of the lower classes in all the Latin American countries," CLASC sent an anguished and impassioned open letter to Pope Paul VI* in which it protested its exclusion and cautioned the Pope against listening only to those "who are satisfied with wealth and who always speak of gradual and peaceful evolution and say . . . that we should be

---

[2] At its fourteenth regular meeting, held in November 1972 in Sucre, Bolivia, CELAM moved to terminate its heavy reliance on foreign financial support (the German Catholic Adveniat, the U.S. Catholic Conference, and the Vatican) and to receive its funds solely from twenty-three national conferences. It also vigorously rebutted attacks by conservatives in Church, government, and private circles that its pastoral programs for the poor favor Marxist ideas. See *The Pilot* (Boston), December 9, 1972.
*See Appendix, p. 86.

patient.'' They complained that

> when some labor union leaders asked that representatives of popular organizations of factory and farm workers be invited, your princes of the Church answered that they 'did not want elements of conflict in this conference of Medellín.' And you know they are right. We are indeed agents of conflict, because for a long time we have represented action beyond words and militant revolutionary obligation beyond verbosity.[3]

Although he made no direct reply to the CLASC letter, the Pope did indirectly respond during his visit to Colombia in conjunction with the Medellín conference. In speeches on the occasion of Development Day and to a group of peasants, and in his conference address, the Pope expressed his profound respect for the poor and pledged to defend their rights; he stressed the importance of education and unionization, exhorted the people to have patience and Christian hope, and condemned violence; and he supported gradual reform, dialogue, and collaboration among all classes.[4]

In fact, the outcome of the Medellín conference was far from what might have been expected.[*] The working papers drafted preparatory to the conference by the Brazilian bishops and their advisers at the request of CELAM took far-reaching positions on the inhuman treatment of the workers and peasants, and on their right to participate in decision-making in the enterprise, the State, and the Church. The two greatest departures from past Church pronouncements were the admission of the theological legitimacy of violence as an instrument of social change and the explicit condemnation of United States "imperialism."[5] The working papers

> explicitly defined the 'Latin American reality' as one of institutionalized violence, a state of 'tyranny' maintained from within by national oligarchies and from without by 'imperialism.' In such circumstances the Thomistic doctrine of justifiable revolution could be invoked.[6]

The Medellín document made no mention of Marxism, either approvingly or disapprovingly. However,

> it did affirm that if peaceful change was not forthcoming, violent change was necessary. It identified Christian commitment in theological terms with commitment to socio-economic change instead of

---

[3] *Iglesia Latinoamericana: ¿Protesta o Profecía?* (Avellaneda, Argentina: Ed. Busqueda, 1969), p. 89.

[4] The speeches of Pope Paul VI are reprinted in the Medellín Conference documents, Second General Conference of Latin American Bishops, *The Church in the Present-Day Transformation of Latin America in the Light of the Council* (Bogotá: General Secretariat of CELAM, 1970), Vol. II (Conclusions), pp. 257-59, 264-67.

[5] David E. Mutchler, *The Church as a Political Factor in Latin America* (New York: Frederick A. Praeger, 1971), pp. 98-130; see also the Medellín Conference documents, *op. cit.*, Vol. I (Position Papers) and Vol. II (Conclusions).

[6] Mutchler, *op. cit.*, p. 111.

[*] See Appendix, pp. 87-89.

merely to personal spiritual conversion.[7]

While the reaction of the majority of the bishops (except for the Brazilians and Chileans) to the working document was highly critical, the conference rejected a substitute draft prepared by the Colombians, in which "they stressed the role of (Christian) labor unions in helping workers 'maintain their dignity.'"[8] The Brazilian-drafted document, which had been widely publicized in the press prior to the opening of the conference, was adopted substantially unchanged after lengthy debate.

A counterpart to the workers' distrust of the Church's motives is the suspicion on the part of some elements within the Church of the unions themselves. Many of the progressive priests regard the unionized workers as a privileged class, not interested in risking their positions to fight for the betterment of the great mass of unemployed or underemployed workers and peasants. Adolfo Bonilla, former Secretary General of CLASC for Central America, acknowledges that the Latin American union movement contains "privileged groups of workers," chiefly in the key economic sectors of the oil, sugar, copper, and banana industries, who are said to isolate themselves from the non-unionized masses and to improve their own status at their expense.[9]

The effectiveness of the labor movement as an instrument of change is further weakened in many cases by its politicization. Labor union leaders' links with political parties and governments have often led to charges that unions are little more than instruments of political policy, and have rendered the leaders themselves susceptible to bribery and corruption. Such was the case of Ángel Borlenghi in Argentina under Perón;[10] of the Mexican Peronist, Luis Morones;[11] and of the *Pelegos* ("those who have sold out") in Brazil under Vargas.[12]

The case of Chile provides a useful illustration of the attitude of the progressive clergy toward the union movement. Under the Christian Democratic regime of Eduardo Frei unions were very active, and strikes and union conflict were common, resulting in considerable loss of revenue.[13] Under the Marxist regime of Salvador Allende, the "government of the workers" attempted to put an end to strikes, and to consolidate the union movement in CUTCh

---

[7]*Ibid.*

[8]*Ibid.*, p. 134.

[9]In Samuel Shapiro, ed., *Integration of Man and Society in Latin America* (Notre Dame, Indiana: University of Notre Dame Press, 1967), p. 89.

[10]Robert J. Alexander, *Labor Relations in Argentina, Brazil and Chile* (New York: McGraw-Hill, 1962), pp. 184-85.

[11]Majorie R. Clark, *Organized Labor in Mexico* (Chapel Hill, North Carolina: University of North Carolina Press, 1934), pp. 109-10.

[12]Alexander, *Labor Relations in Argentina, Brazil and Chile,* pp. 65, 75.

[13]In 1965 political strikes sabotaged Frei's agrarian reform; see Victor Alba, *Politics and the Labor Movement in Latin America* (Stanford, California: Stanford University Press, 1968), p. 254.

(United Chilean Workers' Central) under Communist leadership. In 1971 the Communists sabotaged a strike called by the non-Communist unions in the copper industry, an action that cost them several subsequent union elections.[14]

During a strike at the Exotica copper mine in 1972 an infuriated Allende lashed out at the workers: "I have not lacked the guts to fight against the right wing and imperialism. I will not lack the guts to make some irresponsible workers understand that they cannot demand the impossible." With the strike by the mine drillers in its fifteenth day, threatening to stop all Exotica operations, Allende declared that he might be forced to decree the resumption of work "because the workers are not always right, and this is one of those instances. . . . Tighten your belts and act like responsible Chilean workers."[15]

President Allende frequently reiterated his contention that since the workers "are the government" their attitude toward labor relations should be different from before. Workers' demands should be formulated in a way that reflected the fact that workers were "incorporated in the leadership of the enterprise" and represented on union-management committees.[16] In the Exotica case Allende called for raising the minimum wage and for a percentage of the firm's surplus profits to go to the union. The balance, he stipulated, should be divided between reinvestment by the firm to maintain technological progress, and social investments in the workers in the form of salaries and benefits, "because the copper enterprises are Chile's wages, and the copper workers are the owners of these enterprises when they become part of the process."[17] Yet in April 1973 workers at the El Teniente copper mine went out on an extended

---

[14]See Allende's speech to the Chuquicamata miners, *El Siglo* (Santiago), March 3, 1972, and Allende's speeches on May 1 and on the anniversary of the UP victory, *El Siglo,* November 4, 1971. Significantly, James Petras reported that all the trade unionists he interviewed throughout Chile maintained that the unions should be autonomous and have the right to strike. One Socialist union leader stated: "The day we lose the right to strike I will stop supporting the government." In James Petras, ed., *Latin America: From Dependence to Revolution,* (New York: John Wiley & Sons, 1973), p. 51. See also U.S. Department of Labor, Bureau of Labor Statistics, "The Allende Government Seeks Stronger Base in Organized Labor," *Labor Developments Abroad,* January 1972.

[15]*El Siglo* (Santiago), March 4, 1972.

[16]*El Siglo* (Santiago), November 4, 1971.

[17]*Ibid.* The Allende government also experienced some disaffection by the unionized peasants, who manifested their impatience with the pace and administration of land reform by carrying out illegal land seizures. The Minister of Interior, José Toha, on February 13, 1971, warned the Movimiento Izquierdista Revolucionario (Revolutionary Leftist Movement—MIR) and other extremist groups that such illegal land seizures would not be tolerated because they delay agrarian reform, create disorder, and play into the hands of those who oppose the Chilean revolution. During the Allende period three Chilean peasant labor confederations also conducted lawful strikes for better wages and improved working conditions. These were El Triunfo Campesino, a Marxist organization which claimed 47,600 members in 1969; Ranquil, affiliated with the Chilean Communist Party, which had 31,000 members; and La Libertad, organized by the Christian Democratic Party, with 23,000 members. See U.S. Dept. of Labor, Bureau of Labor Statistics, "Activities of Agrarian Unions and Government Reaction (Chile)" *Labor Developments Abroad,* August 1971. On the attitudes of Chilean agrarian workers, see also James Petras, "Nationalization, Socio-Economic Change, and Popular Participation," in Petras, ed., *Latin America: From Dependence to Revolution,* pp. 4iff.

strike, one in the long series of labor disputes that contributed to the ultimate overthrow of the Allende government.

The Movement of Christians for Socialism,* a group of eighty priests led by the Chilean Jesuit Gonzalo Arroyo, censures those workers

> who favor change and even look forward to benefiting from it, nonetheless are not actively joining the process. The unity of all workers, however, whatever their party option, is necessary at this unique opportunity that is offered to our fatherland for getting rid of the present dependent capitalist system and advancing the cause of the working class throughout Latin America.[18]

In the space of a few years, Fr. Arroyo has transformed the former Christian orientation of the Jesuit labor apostolate into a Marxist one. The work of the Chilean Jesuits in organizing and assisting the workers and peasants dates from 1914, when Fr. Fernando Vives founded the taxi drivers' union; this was followed by unions of seamstresses and of women employees in business enterprises. The opposition of conservative Catholics forced Fr. Vives twice to leave Chile. His successor, Fr. Fernández Pradel, was responsible for the education of numerous future leaders, including Eduardo Frei, who in 1938 broke with the Conservative Party to form the Falange Nacional, the forerunner of the Christian Democratic Party.

The foremost of these socially concerned Jesuits was Fr. Alberto Hurtado, who in 1947 founded the ASICh (Acción Sindical Chilena) to train Christian trade unionists. Fr. Hurtado conceived of the trade union movement as apolitical but committed to seeking thoroughgoing reforms: "Its aspirations are not aimed simply at obtaining some reforms in order to mitigate the present situation of the proletariat but at achieving a reform of the structures in which both capital and labor will have their proper place." The ASICh sought to establish "a Christian social order" and to bring about participation and co-management of the workers in the enterprises.[19]

Fr. Arroyo and his cadre of Christian Marxists reject the possibility of establishing a Christian social order.[20] They dismiss the efforts of Christian Democracy as "a futile, reformist-populist experiment."[21] The "theology of liberation" espoused by the Movement of Christians for Socialism endorses Marxist revolution and urges Christians to join and support it.[22] In a message

---

[18]Press release of April 16, 1971, NADOC #204, May 19, 1971, in LADOC, March 1972.

[19]Alberto Hurtado Cruchaga, *Sindicalismo. Historia, Teoría, Práctica* (Santiago, Chile: Editorial del Pacífico, 1950), pp. 234-36.

[20]See *Time Magazine*, June 5, 1972 and April 23, 1973.

[21]See speech by Fr. Arroyo in Prague, October 1971, in LADOC, January 1972.

[22]*Cristianos por el Socialismo, Primer Encuentro Latinoamericano* (Lima, Peru: CEP, 1972), pp. 28-30, and *¿Una Izquierda Cristiana?* (Lima, Peru: CEP, 1972) pp. 46-47.

*See Appendix, pp. 98-101.

of solidarity on the occasion of the Sixth National CUTCh Congress, the Christians for Socialism declared:

> We believe that Christian workers must . . . join labor unions, and that they in turn must join CUTCh. We reject the notion of founding parallel labor unions, because this weakens the struggle of the working class, not only to have its rights recognized, but also to replace the unjust and inhuman structure of capitalism with a socialist society in which the workers can find just recognition for all.[23]

The position of the Marxist priests of the Movement of Christians for Socialism, as expressed in the document issued at the conclusion of the group's first Latin American regional meeting (Santiago, Chile, April 1972), goes beyond that of CLAT. According to this declaration, political pluralism and dissent, including among leftist groups, should disappear: "The revolutionary process demands that sterile divisions among the leftist groups in Latin America be overcome because they are fomented and used by the imperialists to their advantage." Workers' movements cannot be "fully independent" of the State and political parties because the alliance between Christians and Marxists in the process of liberation is "a strategic alliance which overcomes tactical and opportunistic short-term alliances and means always walking the same path together in a joint political action toward the same historic goal of total liberation."[24]

The priests of the Movement of Christians for Socialism criticize CLAT for being opportunistic. This accusation against Latin American unions is not new and undoubtedly has some validity. However, Robert J. Alexander, long an astute observer of the Latin American labor scene, believes that it would be shortsighted to deny the unions a primary role in the process of Latin American renewal:

> The labor movement in Latin America has not only been interested in so-called 'bread and butter' issues. It has sought to obtain extensive social and labor legislation to protect its members and their organizations. In fact, it has gone beyond this: it has attempted to bring about a basic change in the structure of the Latin American societies.[25]

CLAT's response to the progressive priests' suspicions and distrust of unions in general and of CLAT in particular was voiced by CLAT Secretary General Emilio Máspero: "We appreciate the efforts of these priests for

---

[23]From the Chilean press, December 10, 1971. See also "The Settlement of Labour Disputes in Chile," *International Labour Review,* Vol. 103, No. 4, April 1971.

[24]*Cristianos por el Socialismo,* pp. 15-16.

[25]Robert J. Alexander, *Organized Labor in Latin America* (New York: The Free Press, 1965), p.8. CLAT has also been criticized as being primarily a leadership organization without a significant mass following (except in the Dominican Republic), and for being interested more in social revolution than in hard bargaining with employers. Stiefbold interview with Daniel Montenegro, American Institute for Free Labor Development, April 10, 1973.

11

the liberation of Latin America, but they should not try to tell us how to make the revolution."[26]

Máspero acknowledges that Latin American unions have not always provided effective leadership and that some leaders "prefer the support of the State to that of their own workers." As a result,

> today, a great majority of the Latin American workers distrust the trade unions, whose leaders have not been capable of rising to a moral challenge. . . . Corruption and a bureaucratic approach to leadership have exhausted the sources of idealism both of leaders and workers.[27]

He defends the role of the workers in the Latin American liberation movement, however, pointing to the text of the Caracas Declaration adopted on August 21, 1970 by CLASC delegates from twenty countries attending the Second Union Conference of Latin America, which states that the "workers movement is irreplaceable in a true liberation process," and cautions against confusing the organized workers with the establishment.[28] In identifying the labor movement with the Latin American revolution, Máspero has written:

> Latin America is today in the throes of a revolutionary process. Forces of all kinds are being mobilized either to impede or to advance the revolution. Against this background of social ferment, organized labor is playing an increasingly important role, both among urban and rural workers.[29]

This view is shared by José Gómez Cerda, Secretary General of the Confederación Autónoma de Sindicatos Cristianos (CASC), the CLAT affiliate in the Dominican Republic, who defines the Latin American revolution as "rapid, planned change, in which the working class becomes the actors—rather than the spectators—in shaping their own destiny."[30]

Although CLASC had consistently emphasized that the use of the word "Christian" in its name referred only to a social philosophy and not to the structure or dogma of a particular church, at its congress in Caracas in November 1971 it decided to change its name to Latin American Workers' Central (CLAT). The reason for this shift, in addition to a desire to broaden its appeal, was its intention of highlighting the importance of the worker *per se,* rather than merely the organized workers and the trade unions, in Latin America's liberation. The manifesto of the congress,* issued on November

---

[26]Floridi interview with Emilio Máspero, Caracas, September 8, 1971.

[27]Emilio Máspero, "Latin America's Labor Movement of Christian Democratic Orientation as an Instrument of Social Change," in William V. D'Antonio and Frederick B. Pike, *Religion, Revolution and Reform* (New York: Frederick A. Praeger, 1964), pp. 167 and 170.

[28]*CLASC* (Caracas), September-October 1970, No. 33, pp. 6-7.

[29]Máspero, *op.cit.,* p. 163.

[30]Stiefbold interview with Gómez Cerda, Santo Domingo, August 21, 1973.

*See Appendix, pp. 89-92.

22, 1971, rejects capitalism as "wholly unacceptable for workers and the people," and declares:

> *We workers accept our responsibility . . . of devising a new society*
> . . . where ownership of the means of production will be in the hands
> of the workers. . . . A new society based on the guarantee of freedom
> . . . which will permit (1) political pluralism and dissent to exist . . .
> and (2) a Workers' Movement to be organized, fully independent
> of the state, of political parties, and of any agencies not voicing the
> interests of the working class.[31]

Thus, although the "new society" outlined by CLAT implies a Socialist structure (the manifesto does not state so directly), freedom of individuals and groups is strongly affirmed. Máspero's rejection of the Communist model is explicit:

> The Communists want to introduce into Latin America trade union
> doctrines, ideas, tactics, and objectives that are products of a special
> situation in Russia, a strange and distant country. The attempts of
> Communists to use their own solutions for the problems of Latin
> America serve only to agitate and to hinder the development of an
> authentic and powerful union movement in the service of the
> revolution.[32]

According to Emilio Máspero, the Catholic Church suffers from what might be called a "credibility gap"— inconsistency between words and deeds.[33] He cites the banning of the JOC (Catholic Working Youth), where he and other Catholic union leaders were trained, by certain bishops who considered it too liberal, as evidence of the divorce between Church and labor in Latin America. The greatest hindrance to Church effectiveness, in Máspero's view, is paternalism. The protracted dispute between Máspero and Father Vicente Andrade Valderama, S.J., former national coordinator of Colombian Catholic Social Action, whom Máspero accuses of paternalism, underscores the crisis and the various points of friction between the Church and Catholic labor unions in Latin America.

To understand this dispute, it is necessary to review briefly the history of the labor movement in Colombia. In 1944 the Colombian bishops decided to establish a Catholic labor union, and Father Andrade was entrusted with this task.[34] On June 12, 1946, various Catholic organizations, such as UTRAN (Unión de Trabajadores de Antioquía), UTRABO (Unión de Trabajadores de Boyaca), FEDEMI (Federación Minera de Cundinamarca), and FANAL (Federación Agraria Nacional) were united in the UTC (Unión de Trabaja-

---

[31]NADOC No. 238, January 26, 1972, in LADOC, March 1972.

[32]Máspero, *op. cit.,* p. 175.

[33]Floridi interview with Emilio Máspero, Caracas, September 8, 1971.

[34]Jaime Robayo Rodríguez, *Las Organizaciones de Trabajadores a la Luz de las Doctrinas Sociales de la Iglesia Católica* (Bogotá, Colombia: Universidad Javeriana, 1962), pp. 137ff. and William M. Barbieri, S.J., "Latin America's New Breed," *The Sign* (Catholic monthly), April 1965, p. 18.

dores Colombianos), which today comprises 68.3 per cent of Colombian organized labor. Although only laymen were signatories of the founding act of the UTC, Article 3 of its bylaws expressed its adherence to the principles of Catholic social doctrine. The UTC successfully extended its organization throughout the country, and recorded numerous achievements in the struggle for improved working conditions, higher wages, and progressive social legislation.[35]

Father Andrade and the other clerical advisers of the UTC tried to keep the union out of the political battles between liberals and conservatives.[36] In 1951, when union President Víctor Duarte attempted to mobilize the union's political support behind conservative President Laureano Gómez, he was expelled from the union.[37] In 1957 Tulio Cuevas, president of UTRAVAL (Unión de Trabajadores del Valle), was also expelled for collaborating with the dictator, Gustavo Rojas Pinilla, and with the Colombian Peronists in the CNT (Confederación Sindical de Trabajadores de Colombia).[38]

Unlike in the past when the priest-advisers interfered directly in union affairs, today they limit their involvement to social and religious instruction, leaving the decision-making responsibility to the union leaders and rank-and-file. Today the UTC, FANAL, and UCONAL (National Cooperatives Union) are loosely linked in SETRAC (Selection of Colombian Workers), directed by Fr. Andrade, which instructs trade unionists in Catholic thought. Church ties with the urban-based UTC have greatly diminished, as that union has become sufficiently strong in numbers and influence to assert its independence.[39] Fr. Andrade regrets certain trends within the UTC — its personalism, careerism, and politicization — which he believes are damaging to the union.[40]

Initially the relationship between Fr. Andrade and the UTC on the one hand and CLASC (Latin American Confederation of Christian Trade Unions) on the other was cordial. The UTC participated in the 1954 CLASC founding conference in Santiago, Chile,[41] although it did not join because of its own affiliation with ORIT (CLASC espouses Latin Americanism as opposed to

[35]Moisés Troncoso Poblete and Ben G. Burnett, *The Rise of the Latin American Labor Movement* (New Haven: College and University Press, 1962), p. 35.

[36]Gustavo Lozano Gutiérrez, *El Sindicalismo Colombiano ante la Doctrina Social de la Iglesia* (Bogotá: Univ. Javeriana, 1960), pp. 38ff.

[37]For Duarte's accusations against Fr. Andrade, see *El Nacional* (Bogotá), May 15 and August 11, 1951.

[38]*Revista Javeriana* (Bogotá), May 1954, p. 86; February 1955, pp. 20-21; March 1955, p. 38; Benjamin E. Haddox, *Sociedad y Religión en Colombia* (Bogotá: Ed. Tercer Mundo and the Facultad de Sociología of the Universidad Nacional, 1965), p. 112; and Poblete and Burnett, *op cit.*, p. 85.

[39]Floridi interview with Fr. Andrade, September 29, 1971.

[40]Mutchler, *op. cit.*, p. 162.

[41]Juan Arcos, *El Sindicalismo en América Latina* (Bogotá: Freres, 1964), p. 20.

ORIT's inter-Americanism). But animosity replaced the cordiality when, in 1961, CLASC took advantage of a conflict among the leaders of the UTC in Antioquía to establish the first CLASC affiliate in Colombia, the Asociación Sindical Antioqueña (ASA). Fr. Andrade deplored this action and denounced CLASC's tactics, which, he claimed, included purchasing support with cash.[42] As Mutchler explains:

> CLASC has a reputation among Jesuits in Colombia of being 'leftist.' At any rate, it is regarded by the UTC as a competitor. CLASC attempts to organize Colombian labor had been resisted violently by Colombian bishops, who termed it 'Marxist,' and by Colombian Jesuits, who warned that it would 'divide' the Christian-inspired labor movement.[43]

The Archbishop of Medellín, Tulio Botero Salazar, officially declared that the UTC was the only Colombian Catholic labor union and forbade the priests to associate with the ASA. Fr. Andrade appealed to the International Confederation of Christian Trade Unions (now the World Confederation of Labor) to compel CLASC to cease its divisive activities, but without success.

The support given to the ASA by Fr. Camilo Torres and by the radical priests of Golconda (see Chapter Three) brought more adhesions to CLASC, which succeeded in establishing itself in Colombia on a national level through the Asociación Sindical de Colombia (ASICOL). CLASC sympathized with Camilo Torres, although it did not approve of his decision to resort to violence.[44] It terms the charge that it is guilty of encouraging violence "an egregious lie," and insists that it "seeks revolution in Latin America through peaceful means if possible." It emphatically affirms, however, that, "while non-violent," it "will always be militant, especially in the face of the *de facto* violence of misery."[45]

The points of dispute between these two leaders of Latin American Christian unionism, Emilio Máspero and Fr. Andrade, are both ideological and pragmatic. According to Máspero, Fr. Andrade does not accurately interpret the "signs of the times," because he believes in pan-Americanism, as embodied in ORIT, and denies the necessity of revolution and socialism for Latin America. CLAT sees itself as a "third way" for Latin American unionism, between United States domination (through ORIT) and communism.[46] As a sympathetic priest observed:

> CLASC distrusts the vast North American resources for Latin American labor organizations; it believes that they . . . neutralize

---

[42]Vincente Andrade, "Labor in Latin America," *America* (New York), January 25, 1964, pp. 142-44.

[43]Mutchler, *op. cit.*, p. 152.

[44]Francis, *op. cit.*, p. 600.

[45]Francis, *op. cit.*, p. 600, quoting "The Real CLASC and the False Image Makers," *CLASC* (Santiago), March 1966, p. 6.

[46]Francis, *op. cit.*, p. 602.

and divide the Latin American trade unions . . . CLASC must also struggle against the Communist influence whether this comes from the Soviet Union, Peking, or its Cuban satellite.[47]

CLAT believes that "the true nature of the problems confronting the Latin American working man does not stem from low wages, but rather from the unjust social and economic system in which he operates." Therefore, "the 'superficial' concentration on immediate issues sidetracks organized labor from its 'most profound economic, social, and political objectives,'"[48] i.e., the total transformation of existing structures. The combined force of workers and peasants will be used to "carry out rapid and radical changes, or, in other words, to carry out the revolution."[49]

The new structures envisaged by CLAT will be based on a system of communal enterprise, which would allow private ownership of personal possessions. In the economic sphere, cooperation would replace free competition, with the workers participating in and sharing decision-making responsibility for the enterprises.

According to Emilio Máspero, Pope Paul VI has admitted at least the theoretical legitimacy of non-Marxist socialism (in his apostolic letter to Cardinal Maurice Roy on the eightieth anniversary of *Rerum Novarum*[50], but then in practice has regretted the choice of socialism by Catholics. In this contradiction he sees evidence of continued Church paternalism. Fr. Andrade, conversely, believes that a careful study of the papal documents reveals that such a "compromise" is impossible.[51]

There is no doubt that the social doctrine of the Church has undergone a great evolution. However, papal encyclicals and other ecclesiastical documents are frequently quoted by proponents of divergent views to support their positions. This is in part because, in an effort to avoid the paternalism of the past, the Church today leaves more freedom of choice in practical matters to its followers, taking into account the diverse political and social milieus in which they live. From this stems the crisis which pervades all sectors of the Church, and which is reflected in the relationship of the Church with

---

[47]Fr. José Francisco Corta, S.J., *SIC* (Caracas) July-August, 1969.

[48]Francis, *op. cit.,* p. 598.

[49]Corta, *op. cit.*

[50]*Octogesima Adveniens* (May 14, 1971), St. Paul edition (Boston).

[51]*SETRAC Boletín* (Bogotá), July 1971, No. 114, pp. 1-2; Fr. Bartolomeo Sorge, S. J., reaches the same conclusion in *La Civiltà Cattolica* (Rome), September 16, 1972, pp. 457-70, and November 4, 1972 (pp. 214-29). Significantly, Pope Paul strongly criticized the decision of the Christian Association of Italian Workers (ACLI) in 1969-70 to break with the Christian Democratic Party and to support socialism: "We have . . . deplored (without interfering with their freedom) that the leaders of ACLI have decided . . . to qualify it politically, particularly towards the left, with all the questionable and dangerous implications on the doctrinal and social level." *L'Osservatore Romano* (Vatican City), June 19, 1971.

labor. A brief recapitulation of the essential points of the Church's social doctrine will serve to clarify some of the issues in dispute.

FROM THE "WORKERS' QUESTION" TO THE PROBLEM OF JUSTICE IN THE WORLD

On May 15, 1891, in his pathbreaking encyclical *Rerum Novarum,* Pope Leo XIII expounded the principles of a just solution to the "workers' question." Contrary to the prevailing ideas of economic liberalism, which viewed worker problems purely in economic terms, Leo XIII stressed their moral and religious implications, and the Church's consequent right to intervene in their resolution. The Pope called the suffering of the working masses shameful and inhuman, the result of the greed of the wealthy, and, while not condemning capitalism and rejecting socialism, he censured the abuses of capitalists in the name of human dignity. He advocated unions and associations of both a corporative or mixed nature (including both workers and employers) and of workers alone. This endorsement of worker-only associations was of decisive importance to the future development of the Catholic union movement. However, in Latin America, which had just emerged from colonialism and slavery, social consciousness, even among the clergy, was generally rare.[52] Failure to grasp the true meaning of the encyclical was evident in a contemporary commentary by the Archbishop of Santiago, Mariano Casanova, who asserted that social problems were caused by the refusal of the poor to accept existing differences between the social classes as just and normal.[53]

Pope Pius X (1903-1914) subsequently tried to force Catholics to join strictly confessional workers' associations which were under the direct control of the bishops and the clergy, thus exposing the Catholic unions to charges of paternalism and clericalism. However, faced with the growing difficulty of organizing confessional labor unions, Pius XI (*Quadragesimo Anno,* 1931) stressed the creation of Catholic parallel associations, such as Catholic Action, which were not to have union or political functions, but were to confine themselves to the religious instruction of the workers.

---

[52]Arístides Galvani, "The Christian Ethos in Socioeconomic Development," in Samuel Shapiro, *Cultural Factors in Inter-American Relations* (Notre Dame, Indiana: University of Notre Dame Press, 1968), pp. 227-34; Nelson Werneck Sodre; *A Ideologia do Colonialismo. Seus Reflexos no Pensamento Brasileiro,* (Rio de Janeiro: Ed. Civ. Brasileira, 1965), p. 206; Gilberto Freyre, *The Masters and the Slaves* (New York: Alfred A. Knopf, 1964).

[53]Sergio Ossa Pretot, "Latin America's Plea for Vast Social Change," in John J. Considine, *The Church in the New Latin America* (Notre Dame, Indiana: Fides Publishers, 1964), p. 42; Archbishop Casanova's admonition to the poor to accept their situation is also reported by Frederick C. Pike, "The Catholic Church and Modernization in Peru and Chile." *Journal of International Affairs,* Vol. XX, No. 2, 1966, p. 286.

Reacting to the postwar expansion of communism in Eastern Europe and its penetration of Western European parties and labor unions, Pope Pius XII opposed the closed shop requirement that workers join a particular union, and also denied that participation in management was a "right" of the workers.

Pope John XXIII was less interested in local situations and took a more universal and less doctrinaire approach to workers' problems. In the encyclical *Mater et Magistra* (1961), he stressed the existence of a "greater awareness among workers, as members of unions, of the principal issues in economic and social life." He regarded unions as more than mere instruments of struggle, and, without deciding whether or not it was their right, approved the workers' desire to be "partners" in their places of work. With John XXIII Catholics had more freedom to associate across religious lines. In the encyclical the Pope praised not only Catholic associations and unions, but also non-confessional ones. In *Pacem in Terris* (1963), which was directed beyond the Catholic world to "all men of good will," the Pope enumerated the gains gradually won by the working classes in economic and public affairs as one of the "three distinctive characteristics" of our age:

> Today . . . workers all over the world refuse to be treated as if they were irrational objects without freedom, to be used at the arbitrary disposition of others. They insist that they be always regarded as men with a share in every sector of human society. . . .[54]

Many people have interpreted some of Pope John's declarations and actions as revolutionary. But some of these interpretations have exceeded his intentions. There is no doubt, however, that the pontificate of John XXIII caused a crisis in all sectors of the Church, including the labor sector. This is particularly valid for Latin America. The Colombian guerrilla-priest Camilo Torres once affirmed:

> I do not care if the big press continues to call me a Communist. I prefer to follow my conscience rather than bend before the pressures of the oligarchy. I would rather follow the rules of the pontiffs of the Church than those of our ruling class. John XXIII authorizes me to march along with the Communists.[55]

Torres' reference to Pope John overlooks the fact, however, that in *Pacem in Terris* the latter had specifically rejected violence by quoting Pius XII: "Salvation and justice are not to be found in revolution, but in evolution through concord. Violence has always achieved only destruction and not construction."

The Council Vatican II (1962-1965) and Pope Paul VI have pursued the policy of John XXIII, giving indirect attention to labor within the context

---

[54]*Pacem in Terris* (April 11, 1963), St. Paul edition (Boston).
[55]Frente Unido, September 1965, quoted in Norberto Habegger, *Camilo Torres Prete e Guerrigliero*, (Florence, Italy. Cultura Editrice, 1968), p. 71.

of the problems of peace and justice in the world. The Council document *On the Church in the Modern World* declared: "Among the basic rights of the human person must be counted the right of freely founding labor unions." It also approved of the strike as "a necessary, though ultimate, means for the defense of the workers' own rights and the fulfillment of their just demands."[56]

An important step with regard to the Catholic labor movement was the Council's decision to approve, in addition to associations directly administered by the hierarchy (such as those affiliated with Catholic Action), forms of apostolate independent of Church paternalism, which are more compatible with the contemporary pluralistic world. As a result, several organizations eliminated the words "Catholic" or "Christian" from their names. For example, the International Confederation of Christian Trade Unions became the World Confederation of Labor. In some cases only the name was changed but in others the change was more profound and Catholicism and Christianity remain only as sources of inspiration of a vaguely defined humanism.

It is significant that in his apostolic letter, *The Coming Eightieth* (May 14, 1971), commemorating the eightieth anniversary of the encyclical of Leo XIII, Pope Paul VI devotes only one paragraph to the workers, in which he urges them to put the common good before their own, and not to abuse the right to strike. For Pope Paul, apparently, the workers' question has lost its former importance, because of the more urgent problems of justice in the world. Indeed, he seems to consider unionized workers a privileged group who should be willing to make sacrifices for those less fortunate. The Pope does not offer any blueprint for the new model of society he invokes, however, thus deepening the crisis of Catholic institutions. Now it is more difficult to refer to papal decisions for specific guidelines, because of the great latitude left to individuals. However, one must ask, will Catholics be united in their political choices? And, once made, will the Pope accept them? The charge of contradiction leveled by Emilio Máspero against Pope Paul VI stems precisely from this dilemma.

---

[56]Walter Abbot, *The Documents of Vatican II* (New York: Guild Press, 1966), pp. 276-78.

II
BETWEEN REFORM AND THE CLASS STRUGGLE

The solutions advocated by Catholics to the problems of Latin America, particularly the problems of the workers and peasants, range from moderate reform to drastic overthrow of existing structures (with or without violence); from an indigenous Latin American, humanist, and Christian socialism, to a collectivism that accepts many Marxist features, alliance with the Communists, and, in a few cases, dictatorship.

In this chapter we begin to examine the conflict between these trends in Mexico, Brazil, Costa Rica, Panama, Chile, and Peru. In particular, we will analyze some of the causes of the transition by some clergy and laymen from a reformist approach to one based on class struggle: (1) the reappraisal of Marxism; (2) the adoption of the technique of *conscientização* (consciousness-raising), i.e., learning to perceive social, political, and economic contradictions and to act against oppression; and (3) the frustration over the alleged failure of both Christain Democracy and community development programs as alternatives to capitalism and communism.

In the history of Latin American workers' movements, unions of Christian or Catholic inspiration were preceded by secular ones, which were strongly influenced by the anarchism, social class polarization, and anticlericalism imported by the European immigrants. They were not, with the possible exception of Mexico, an outgrowth of a popular and industrial revolution, as in the United States, but were conceived (as they still largely are) as the expression of "revolutionary" ideologies and parties, and as the vehicles for bringing about a sociopolitical revolution; almost without exception they were contrary to Church doctrine. This accounts for the ethico-religious, inter-class, reformist, and assistance-oriented nature of the Catholic workers' associations born in Latin America following the first social encyclical (*Rerum Novarum,* 1891). In recent decades, however, this conservative orientation of the Catholic Church has begun to change, with respect to both politics and the unions. As J. Lloyd Mecham wrote in his classic work on the relationship between Church and State in Latin America: "The identification of Roman Catholicism with conservatism seems to be disappearing."[1]

Today parties and unions of Christian inspiration affirm their commitment to change under the rubric of "Christian Democracy." In fact, some of their spokesmen go so far as to term the Christian Democratic movement "revolutionary." One must be careful about taking such rhetoric at face value,

---

[1]J. Lloyd Mecham, *Church and State in Latin America,* rev. ed. (Chapel Hill: The University of North Carolina Press, 1966), p. 425.

21

however. What the Christian Democrats actually intend by the "communitary socialism" they advocate is "some sort of participatory, communitary democracy."[2] Eduardo Frei's agrarian reform and nationalizations in Chile as well as Rafael Caldera's "Venezuelization" of oil are an extension of the ideas of Christian and communitary democracy and personalism elaborated in France by Jacques Maritain and Emmanuel Mounier.[3]

Some of these ideas have undergone mutation when applied in the Latin American context, however. This is particularly true in the case of the Latin American priests active in politics and in workers' organizations, who drew their inspiration from the Belgian priest Joseph Cardijn (later appointed cardinal by Pope John XXIII, and founder of the JOC) and also from the French worker-priests.[4] The innovative worker-priest movement, after some years of confusion, became institutionalized and immune to Communist penetration. But when transplanted to Latin America it underwent a serious crisis due to the more volatile economic and political environment and the dearth of sophisticated anticommunist interpreters of Marxism of the stature of some Europeans, such as Jean-Paul Sartre. Thus, in many instances, the revolutionary priests of Latin America were absorbed by the united fronts they joined with the Communists, and turned against the Christian Democrats.

In sum, the three currents within the Catholic apostolate posited in Chapter One — "centrist-reformist," "leftist-reformist," and "radical revolutionary" — are engaged in an ideological and practical test of strength in Latin America. Examples in this and the following chapter will illustrate the positions and influence of some of the individuals and movements within this necessarily somewhat schematic taxonomy.

MEXICO

The weakness of the Catholic labor organization in Mexico is primarily due to three factors which characterize the Church and labor scene. The first is the legacy of Church-State conflict and the resulting importance of the separation of the two. The second is the existence of large, catch-all labor organizations which are both dependent on, and supportive of, the dominant political party. The third and related factor is the pluralistic tolerance of a wide range of ideological diversity within these "official" unions, which

---

[2]This view was elaborated in the Venezuelan Jesuit magazine *SIC* (Caracas), April 1970.

[3]In his last book, *Le Paysan de la Garonne,* Maritain strongly protested the "temporalization" of Christianity, i.e., its reduction to a mere "earthly social" value.

[4]Joseph Cardijn, "De la JOC à la Mission," in Emile Poulat, *Naissance des Prêtres-Ouvriers* (Tournai, Belgium: Casterman, 1965), pp. 138ff.

mitigate separatist tendencies, and lessen the attractiveness to workers of joining separate, Church-supported unions.

The first Mexican Catholic Conference (1903), following the teachings of Pope Leo XIII, committed itself to organizing the workers into federations, under the direction of parish priests. The early Catholic organizations emphasized mutual aid, shorter working hours, and prohibition of child labor.[5] These organizations—the association of Operarios Guadalupanos (1905), the Unión Católica Obrera (1908), the Confederación de Círculos Obreros Católicos (1912), the Federación Nacional Católica del Trabajo (1917), and the Liga Nacional Católica de la Clase Media and Liga Nacional Católica Campesina (1925)—had to contend with the hostility of the revolutionary and anti-clerical governments, which banned Catholic schools and political parties, confiscated Church properties, and denied the clergy the right to vote. By 1925 the Confederación Nacional Católica del Trabajo (CNCT) grouped about 400 unions. Most organized workers, however, though considering themselves Catholic, were affiliated either with the Confederación Regional de Obreros Mexicanos (CROM), which was then allied with the government, or with the Communist Confederación General de Trabajadores (CGT), until the formation of the Confederación de Trabajadores de Mexico (CTM) in 1936, which, through its close ties with the governing Partido Revolucionario Institucional (PRI), became—and has remained—the dominant labor organization.[6] All Church organizations were submerged in the Church-State conflict of 1926-29, and only surfaced again at the sufferance of the government.[7]

The Jesuit Centro Laboral, located in a lower-class section of Mexico City (Colonia Argentina), is one of these organizations. Its projects include an elementary school, two vocational schools, a sports program, a house for religious retreats for workers, and the Liga Guadalupana de Obreros, which sends priests to factories to conduct religious services. The vocational schools enjoy an excellent reputation in the city and the young mechanics and printers it graduates find immediate employment in the city's firms. The popular sports program, which attracts 1,500 soccer players weekly, has received the support and encouragement of the Mexican soccer team and the National Soccer

[5]See Carlos Casteneda, "Social Development and Movements in Latin America," in Joseph Moody, *Church and Society: Catholic Social and Political Thought and Movements (1789-1950)* (New York: Arts Inc., 1953), p. 771.

[6]Victor Alba, *Politics and the Labor Movement in Latin America* (Stanford, California: Stanford University Press, 1968), pp. 192-94; L. Vincent Padgett, *The Mexican Political System* (Boston: Houghton Mifflin Co., 1966), pp. 87-109; Marjorie R. Clark, *Organized Labor in Mexico* (University of North Carolina Press: Chapel Hill, N.C., 1934), pp. 86-96; and Robert E. Scott, *Mexican Government in Transition* (University of Illinois Press: Urbana, Illinois, 1964), pp. 163-68.

[7]Robert E. Quirk, "Religion and the Mexican Social Revolution," in William V. D'Antonio and Frederick C. Pike, *Religion, Revolution and Reform* (New York: Frederick A. Praeger, 1964), pp. 61-71.

Federation. However, the Centro Laboral, mindful of the history of Church-State conflict in Mexico, refrains from political activity, and devotes its resources exclusively to the spiritual and technical training of the workers and recreational pursuits.

Representing an alternative, politicized, approach is the Juventud Trabajadora de Mexico (JUTRAM—Working Youth of Mexico), directed by a French priest, Fr. Morelli. JUTRAM criticizes the government of President Luis Echeverria; the CTM, whose leaders it charges are imposed from above; and the Catholic Church. It cites the Liga Guadalupana de Obreros as an example of religion being the "opium of the people." It deplores the fact that the Centro Laboral receives aid from North America (through the Jesuits of New Orleans) and from Mexican businessmen,[8] and condemns the Centro's tendency to "divide the oppressed classes" by its exclusive concern with improving the workers' skills without instilling in them a class consciousness and a sense of proletarian solidarity. JUTRAM's goals are: (1) to support the Frente Auténtico del Trabajo (FAT), which is associated with CLAT, and the Acción Cristiana Obrera (ACO), of which JUTRAM is the youth section, in the struggle against U.S. imperialism and the exploitation of the proletariat; (2) to combat the official unions, which it claims accept leadership and direction from the government, do not demonstrate solidarity with opposition labor and peasant organizations, and do not defend student opponents against government reprisals; and (3) to foster united action by workers, peasants, and students, including Communists. In order to avoid the appearance of "parallelism" (i.e. political affiliation with the progressive clergy, as in the case of the Christian unions' ties to the Christian Democrats), JUTRAM creates special departments for youth action in the organizations in which it is active.[9] Among the methods it uses to develop the workers' "critical, political, and revolutionary conscience" is *conscientização,* a consciousness-raising technique that will be discussed later in this chapter.[10]

PANAMA

The hopes of many seeking a viable indigenous Latin American alternative to both capitalism and communism were optimistically pinned on the "com-

[8]Floridi interview with Fr. Morelli, October 1971. On the employers' association, see *La Empresa ante las Exigencias de la Sociedad, Memoria del VI Congreso Nacional USEM,* Mexico City, October 4-6, 1971.

[9]Information based on interview with Fr. Morelli and on JUTRAM manifesto, *Plano de Trabajo de la JUTRAM,* Mexico City, September 28, 1971 (mimeo).

[10]IDOC-International (North American edition), October 16, 1971, pp. 39-44; see also "La Represión del Jueves de Corpus 10 de Julio de 1971: un Testimonio," in *Acción Obrera* (Mexico City), July 1971, p. 5, and September 1971, pp. 2-4.

munity development'' programs that were introduced in Latin America in the 1950's. However, according to the Colombian sociologist Orlando Fals-Borda, this expectation has generally not materialized: ''Little more than a palliative in most countries, the community development campaigns have been emasculated of their intrinsically revolutionary elements and left idle, but fattening, as a supporting element of the status quo.'' While they did accomplish one of their objectives — checking ''subversion'' — they did not effect any fundamental change in traditional attitudes and relationships. The so-called ''natural'' leaders, once elected to the governing boards, either were dismissed if they proved to be too radical, or else were co-opted. Thus, ''once institutionalized, community development became respectable, itself a member of the establishment.''[11]

One such community development program promoted by the Latin American bishops was in San Miguelito, a Panamanian town of 70,000 inhabitants located about twelve miles from the capital. Virtually a squatters' shantytown, ''San Miguelito had acquired the name of a vast disaster area, with a high crime index, almost 100 per cent unemployment, broken homes, prostitution, and organized vice.''[12]

In 1963 five priests from the Chicago archdiocese began work in San Miguelito. They stressed the importance of the laity and the notion of a fundamental renewal. Their successes were notable both in their religious and in their secular undertakings. The high-water mark occurred in October 1968, when a nationwide strike was called to protest the overthrow of the recently elected President, Arnulfo Arias, by a military junta. Nationwide the strike was a failure — except in San Miguelito, where it was nearly 100 per cent effective. Within a month, following a remarkably eloquent peaceful demonstration for restoration of civil rights and liberties by the citizens of San Miguelito, the regime capitulated, and San Miguelito was guaranteed freedom of speech and assembly. In 1971, following the first free elections ever held in the country, the Panamanian President, General Torrijos, stated: ''If every community did what you did, we could not control the country; but had every community in Panama your spirit and were it organized as well as San Miguelito, then our seizure of the government would not have been necessary in the first place.''[13]

---

[11]From Jorge Lara-Braud, ed., *Our Claim on the Future* (New York: Friendship Press, 1970), in LADOC, June 1970.

[12]''A Parish Demands — and Gets — Free Elections under a Dictatorship,'' *Publik* (German Catholic weekly), December 18, 1970, in LADOC, May 1971. The subsequent discussion draws largely on this article. See also Francisco Bravo, *San Miguelito in Panama: Parrocchie nei Cortili* (Milan: Jaca Book, 1968), p. 22 and *passim*.

[13]LADOC, May 1971, *op. cit.*

Only a few months after the December 1970 publication of the article in which these accomplishments were recounted, however, Fr. Hector Gallego, a young Colombian priest who had been active among the Panamanian peasants, was kidnapped and disappeared without a trace. The honeymoon between Panamanian bishops and the government had ended, because of the failure of the civil authorities to investigate the incident and their refusal to permit a foreign board of inquiry. The bishops also protested the authorities' intimidation of the clergy and reprisals against institutions, including the news media, that had defended the position of the Church.

Personally, General Torrijos and the Catholic hierarchy remained on good terms. The bishops were invited to comment on proposed constitutional amendments, which they did on June 27, 1972:

> The peasants, the Indians, and the workers, those who live beyond access to the social benefits, are demanding that legislation be enacted on the basis of their rights. They are in the majority . . . that is demanding from us priority consideration in the constitution. What will we do to give them participation in politics . . . in education . . . in labor affairs? At the present political crossroads . . . we believe it is important to ensure . . . freedom of expression and . . . the right to be informed. . . .[14]

Yet, at precisely the same time, the first edition of the San Miguelito newspaper, *La Verdad,* was confiscated, and a Jesuit magazine, *Social Dialogue,* was fined for "offending Christian morals." At issue in the latter case was a litany of what the priest-editors termed "oppressions": "being without a job . . . having a military officer as president . . . belonging to a phony labor union . . . living under oppression."[15]

Undoubtedly such contradictory developments contribute to the radicalization of progressive Catholic groups, and generate in them mistrust of the Church itself. They criticize the bishops for collaborating with oppressive governments, and conclude that the Church is more interested in spiritual conversion than in rapid transformation of the political structures.

CHILE

One group that thought it had a genuine opportunity to implement Christian social doctrine was the Chilean Christian Democrats.[16] And yet ultimately

---

[14]*La Estrella de Panama,* July 1972. Gen. Torrijos' regime was strengthened in the elections of August 6, 1972.

[15]*The National Catholic Register* (Los Angeles, California), July 9, 1972.

[16]"The Christian Democrats regard themselves explicitly as an 'alternative' to the Marxian parties, speak in a populist, even revolutionary, idiom, and call for a 'revolution in liberty.'" Maurice Zeitlin and James Petras, "The Working Class Vote in Chile: Christian Democracy versus Marxism," in Stanley M. Davis and Louis Wolf Goodman, *Workers and Managers in Latin America* (Lexington, Massachusetts: D.C. Heath and Co., 1972), p. 250.

they, too, were frustrated in their attempt to translate this doctrine into a workable alternative to both capitalism and communism. The story of the evolution of both ecclesiastical and political life in Chile leading up to the election of President Salvador Allende is recounted by the Canadian sociologist-priest Yves Vaillancourt.

In the 1960's, the Chilean Church was considered one of the most progressive in Latin America. Based in the Centro Bellarmino in Santiago, which included the Center for the Economic and Social Development of Latin America (DESAL), headed by the Belgian Jesuit Roger Vekemans, the socially concerned Jesuits seemed to be the impetus behind the official Church's swing to the left. But unlike what was occurring in Colombia and Brazil at that time, it was not only one sector of the Church in Chile, but the whole Church, that seemed to be galvanized.[17] Yet, in reality, the Church's position was ambiguous: while declaring its apolitical intentions, in the 1964 electoral campaign it openly supported the Christian Democrat Eduardo Frei against the candidate of the leftist coalition, Salvador Allende. Thus, "it was clear . . . that the Church identified itself with Christian Democracy and that the struggle became a battle between Christians and Marxists."[18]

The situation prevailing at the time of the 1970 elections was far more complex. Positions within both the clergy and the political sector had become more differentiated. One faction within the Church continued to support Christian Democracy, but significant numbers now favored the rightist Alessandri on the one hand or the leftist Allende on the other. There was also division within the ranks of the socially concerned Jesuits of the Centro Bellarmino. While their publication, *Mensaje,* adopted more radical political positions, the Center for Research and Social Action (CIAS) maintained the "developmentalist" stance of 1964. In sum, writes Vaillancourt:

> with such a spread of opinions in the Church, this electoral campaign was not simply a Christian-Marxist confrontation. It seemed rather to be a struggle engaging reactionary Christians (with Alessandri) reformist Christians (with Tomic and Christian Democracy), and revolutionary Christians (with Allende and his new Popular Unity coalition). That is to say, politically the Church's image was now multi-dimensional.[19]

Caught up in this political struggle was the Latin American Institute for Doctrine and Social Studies (ILADES), another Chilean Jesuit organization. The crisis through which ILADES passed was both a cause and an effect of the weakening of Christian Democracy in Chile, and, in a larger sense,

---

[17]*Vispera* (Montevideo), April 1971, in LADOC, December 1971.
[18]*Ibid.*
[19]*Ibid.*

reflects the major crisis of confidence which the Church is facing today in Latin America.

Again drawing on the work of Fr. Vaillancourt, the principal protagonists within ILADES were its director, Fr. Pierre Bigo, a French Jesuit and author of several books on sociology, Marxism, and Soviet communism; and Fr. Gonzalo Arroyo, the Chilean Jesuit assistant director. The dispute concerned a conflict over which of its two basic components ILADES should emphasize: reflection on social problems and Church social doctrine or social science research into the problems of underdevelopment.

A small minority, aligned with Fr. Bigo, supported the first position. This group interpreted what was transpiring in ILADES as a confrontation between Christians and Marxists. They strenuously objected to the fact that increasing amounts of time were devoted to the study of Marxism as an analytical approach to Latin American problems, with consequently less time devoted to Christian reflection. Moreover, some persons affiliated with ILADES were openly criticizing Church social doctrine and questioning its relevance to contemporary sociopolitical problems. Finally, the Bigo group felt that one of ILADES' greatest merits, its objectivity, was being sacrificed to this growing politicization.

The Arroyo group, on the other hand, viewed the confrontation as a clash between developmentalist Christians and revolutionary Christians. To them the crisis of ILADES, brought about by the effort of those who controlled ILADES to impose their will on the majority of the Institute's professors and students, was, on a small scale,

> an image of the contradictions that affected the Church and Latin American society, which thus had to accept dependence and a situation of domination and exploitation, inasmuch as the decision centers controlling their cultural, political and economic life were located outside them.[20]

More than just denouncing the ambiguities of the Church's social doctrine and its protestations of objectivity, the Arroyo group was evolving a "theology of liberation" to apply to the cause of the liberation of Latin America.[21] Its response to the charge of denuding ILADES of its Christianity and its objectivity is that what it actually opposed was the particular developmentalist choices made by ILADES, which amounted, in effect, to an endorsement of Christian Democracy.

In Vaillancourt's view, "the crisis of ILADES probably was caused less by a shift from the pastoral to the political than by a shift from the reformist

---

[20]*Ibid.*

[21]Gustavo Gutiérrez, "Notes for a Theology of Liberation," *Theological Studies,* June 1970, in LADOC, August 1970.

camp to the revolutionary camp." As long as ILADES favored Christian Democracy, its political ties were not questioned. The trouble began when a significant number of its students and staff defected to the Movement of Unitary Popular Action (MAPU), which supported Allende.

The upshot of the dispute was the resignation of the Arroyo faction from ILADES at the end of 1969, and the victory within the Institute of the developmentalist position.

In 1971 Fr. Arroyo founded the Movement of Christians for Socialism (see Chapter One). At its June 1972 meeting in Santiago, which brought together four hundred participants from all twenty-eight Latin American countries, the Movement of Christians for Socialism declared that, while it did not accept the Marxist doctrines of atheism or materialism, the time had come for "a strategic alliance of revolutionary Christians and Marxists in the process of liberating the continent." "The class struggle," it pronounced, "has so sharpened in Latin America that there remain only two possibilities: dependent capitalism and underdevelopment, or socialism."[22]

Fr. Arroyo and his group regarded their support for the regime of President Salvador Allende as the logical extension of this philosophy. They therefore affirmed that the "coming to power of the Popular Government and its decisive action in favor of the building of socialism represent the hope of the working masses."[23] While not denying the "difficulties and mutual mistrust" of the past, they nevertheless believed that "the evolution that has taken place between Marxists and Christians . . . permits a common action in the historic project to which our country has committed itself."[24] Although they recognized that "obviously, not everything that is being done is positive," the eighty priests who originated the Movement of Christians for Socialism emphasized that criticism of the revolutionary process should come from within, not outside it.[25]

In economic terms, they specifically endorse nationalization of mines and mineral resources, socialization of banks and monopolistic industries, and expansion and extension of agrarian reform. However, for them, socialism is more than just a system of economic organization of society:

> In effect, socialism, characterized by the appropriation by society of the means of production, opens the way to a new economy which makes possible an autonomous and more rapid development, since it overcomes the division of society into antagonistic classes. However, socialism is not only a new economy. It ought also to generate new values which make possible the emergence of a society

---

[22]*Time Magazine*, June 5, 1972, p. 57.
[23]IDOC-International, September 25, 1971.
[24]*Ibid.*
[25]NADOC No. 204, May 19, 1971, in LADOC, March 1972.

more united and fraternal in which the worker assumes the dignity to which he is entitled.[26]

Fr. Beltrán Villegas, Professor of Theology at Catholic University of Santiago, who is favorably disposed to socialism, nonetheless disputes the insistence of the Movement of Christians for Socialism that all Christians accept its particular blueprint for "incarnating the solidarity that the gospel demands."[27] What if, he asks, not all workers can put aside their party affiliations and endorse this "unique opportunity" to eliminate capitalism in Chile?

Fr. Villegas also objects to the priests' "class-based attitude." Although he admits the possible validity of the Marxist concept of the class struggle as an analytical tool, he contends that any Christian who adopts this technique must keep in mind two things:

first, that neither its scientific validity as sociological method nor its separability from the global Marxist theory is universally evident; and second, that the Marxist view of the proletarian class as the exclusive flag-bearer for the future of humanity does not coincide at all with what the gospel means by the blessedness of the poor.[28]

Regarding the priests' censure of the "lack of class consciousness" among "significant groups of workers," Fr. Villegas reiterates:

I consider it *possible,* but extremely risky, to opt for social transformation via the class struggle, and I respect the option you have made. But please say very clearly that it is a political option and that it cannot be held up as a mandatory gospel rule for political activity.[29]

Fr. Villegas also questions the eighty priests' facile progression from a Christian concept of solidarity to socialism, and from there to Marxist socialism; from "a social takeover of the means of production to a State takeover"; and from collaborating with Marxists in a single endeavor to collaborating with them "in the wholesale construction of Marxist socialism."[30]

Subsequent events, including the meeting of the priests with Fidel Castro (November 1971) and their visit to Cuba (February-March 1972), would seem to confirm his analysis of the direction of their thinking. The purpose of their meeting with Castro was to convey a sense of solidarity among Chilean Christians and like-minded revolutionaries from other countries:

The revolution we are committed to is not a parallel or separate one of our own; it is the single, great revolution that is being fought for throughout Latin America, which was victorious in Cuba and is now starting in Chile, inspired by the common struggle of the workers, both Christian and non-Christian.[31]

---

[26]*Ibid.*

[27]*Pastoral Popular* (Santiago monthly), May-June 1971, in LADOC, March 1972.

[28]*Ibid.*

[29]*Ibid.*

[30]*Ibid.*

[31]"The Eighty Priests Meet with Fidel Castro," mimeographed report, November 29, 1971, in LADOC, March 1972.

They expressed their "satisfaction" at Castro's message "on the participation of Christians in the Latin American political process as not only tactical, but also strategic allies."[32]

From Havana the priests issued a message to Latin American Christians,* in which they summoned them to "join all honest men, Christians or not, who are struggling for the liberation of our countries."[33] Concluding their visit, they declared:

> In assessing Cuba, we reaffirm our belief that historically socialism is the only solution for our continent to break . . . the capitalist and imperalist chains of oppression. . . . We believe that in Latin America the time has come to fight and not to talk.[34]

At their annual plenary assembly the Chilean bishops, after having examined the above message of the priests, sent them a letter condemning their call for revolutionary violence and telling them, particularly the foreigners in the group, to refrain from politics or leave the priesthood.

Among the priests of the Movement of Christians for Socialism the divergent views of Fr. Pablo Fontaine deserve special mention. In a letter to Fr. Arroyo, Secretary General of the movement, Fr. Fontaine observes that "the government has, in a short time, engendered too much opposition," and warns that "the confrontation being sought will end, at best, in a Communist dictatorship, which I do not like too much, and at worst, in a Brazilian-style dictatorship." Therefore Fr. Fontaine advocates resumption of dialogue with the Christian Democrats to "prevent the failure of the revolution."[35] Fr. Arroyo, however, did not accept Fr. Fontaine's suggestion of a rapprochement with the Christian Democratic Party.

The Chilean bishops refused to cosponsor or send official representatives to the first Latin American conference of Christians for Socialism, voicing "deep reservations" about the ideology of some of the participants, and reflecting their attitude that the movement goes beyond the legitimate aims and role of the Church. The episcopal commission of CELAM's Social Action Department, convening in Rio de Janeiro in June 1972, some weeks after this meeting, noted:

> Knowing that it is being infiltrated by Marxist tendencies, the Church in Latin America must be most perspicacious. It would do well to analyze very closely the documents of the Christians for Socialism meeting and the repercussions they are having in various countries.[36]

---

[32]*Ibid.*

[33]*La Tribuna* (Santiago), March 6, 1972.

[34]*Ibid.*

[35]*Ercilla* (Santiago), March 15, 1972.

[36]*El Catolicismo* (Bogotá), August 27, 1972, in LADOC, April 1973.

*See Appendix, pp. 98-99.

31

Returning to the original point of departure for this discussion, it is thus obvious that ILADES and the Movement of Christians for Socialism represent two poles of opinion within the socially concerned Latin American clergy today. Likewise, the rupture that led to the creation of Fr. Arroyo's group is a microcosm of the schism within the contemporary Catholic Church.

The advocates of socialism still represent a small but vocal minority among Latin American priests and laymen. Chile's Movement of Priests for Socialism consists of a nucleus of eighty priests out of a national total of some 2,500. The Argentine Movement of Priests for the Third World (see Chapter Three) numbers four hundred, out of a clergy of 5,200. The Mexican Movement of Priests for the People, a newer organization, probably does not have much over one hundred members, out of a clergy of 8,700.[37] Yet their impact far exceeds their numbers, and hence merits our attention.

BRAZIL

One of the questions that concerns these groups is, should structural transformation precede or follow efforts to improve the condition of the workers, enhance the role of the unions, and accomplish social reforms? Fr. Antonio Melo, a Brazilian priest active among the poor farmers of northeast Brazil, advocates the reform approach. Dom Helder Câmara, Archbishop of Olinda and Recife, believes that structural change and "liberation" must precede.

Born in poverty-stricken northeast Brazil in 1909, Dom Helder has long been concerned with the problems of poverty and labor. In the 1930's he endorsed the fascistic Brazilian Integralist Action, which had the backing of workers, students, and other activists. In the early 1960's he supported the Goulart regime's equally unsuccessful reform efforts, which preceded the 1964 coup that brought the military to power.[38] A decade earlier he launched the Crusade of Saint Sebastian in Rio de Janeiro, a fund drive to "put an end to the *favelas* (slums)."[39] The campaign, which was founded on the principle of Christian charity and class harmony, received the support of the city's wealthy citizens.

Today such people might not be part of Dom Helder's natural constituency. Internationally known as an opponent of the status quo, and nominated for

---

[37]*Time Magazine*, June 5, 1972, p. 57.

[38]Frederick C. Turner, *Catholicism and Political Development in Latin America* (Chapel Hill: University of North Carolina Press, 1971), p. 151.

[39]Oriana Fallaci, "Interview with Archbishop Helder Câmara," in *Siete Dias Ilustrados* (Buenos Aires), October 5, 1970, and LADOC, June 1971.

the Nobel Prize, Dom Helder acknowledges that he is a Socialist. However, he is equally critical of the communism of the Soviet Union and China as he is of capitalism:

> I can't see any solution coming from capitalism. But I don't see it either in the Socialist governments that exist today, because they are all based on dictatorships. . . . My socialism is a special one that respects the human person and turns to the gospel. My socialism is justice. Justice doesn't mean making everyone have the same amount of wealth. . . . By justice, I mean a better distribution of goods, nationally and internationally.[40]

Dom Helder calls for an "authentic Marxist effort" that will produce both a new attitude toward religion and a new attitude toward socialism, linked in what he calls "spiritualist socialisms":

> The hour has come for Marxists to review their two assumptions: that religion is alienation, and that socialism is necessarily bound up with dialectical materialism. The hour has come for Christians also, not necessarily to adopt any one system, but at least to recognize the existence of a neo-Marxism that rejects the distortions of socialism and can see in the Christian message a strong inspiration for the full socialization of property, power and knowledge.[41]

Some critics charge that Dom Helder is more theoretician than activist, more interested in consciousness-raising among the workers than in proposing concrete programs. To support this criticism they point to the failure of his 1968 effort to create a nonviolent "Movement of Moral Pressure for Liberation."

To his enemies Dom Helder is a traitor to the Church and to his country. They accuse him of spreading a distorted image of Brazil abroad (because of his denunciation of the torture of political prisoners), of not contributing to Brazil's development effort, and of proselytizing discouragement that leads to subversion. Dom Helder realizes that he represents a minority of the Brazilian episcopacy, and moreover that in the present Brazilian political climate there is little chance of effecting widespread changes. He asserts that his personal rapport with Pope Paul is good, however (perhaps due to his rejection of birth control for Brazil). "The Pope knows perfectly well what I do and what I say," he observes. "And," he continues, "if the Pope thought I am doing wrong by acting as I do, and told me to stop, I would stop."[42]

Dom Helder denies that he is fomenting armed violence; indeed, his tactic of "peaceful violence" can be likened to civil disobedience:

---

[40]*Ibid.*

[41]Acceptance speech upon receiving honorary doctorate from the University of Münster, Germany, June 21, 1972, CIDOC 72/378, in LADOC, March 1973.

[42]Oriana Fallaci, *op. cit.* However, it came as a surprise to many that Dom Helder was not among the approximately thirty new cardinals, including two Brazilians, appointed by Pope Paul in February 1973.

not the violence of arms, but the violence of Gandhi and Martin Luther King, the violence of Christ. I call it violence, because it won't settle for trivial reforms but calls for a complete revolution of the present structures, on socialist bases and without the shedding of blood.[43]

Two local Catholic organizations through which Dom Helder exerts his influence are SORPE (Rural Orientation Service of Pernambuco)[44] and ACO (Catholic Workers' Action) of the Northeast. The latter, with the participation of Dom Helder, in 1967 published a critique of the development programs for the Northeast, entitled "Development without Justice." While acknowledging the region's recent economic progress, this document highlights aspects considered deleterious to the workers: the possibility that industrialization would increase the already great unemployment, and that the existing feudal structure would be replaced by a capitalism that "confronts problems without concerning itself with man" and "makes money the principal goal."[45]

Dom Helder's analysis is in part echoed by one of his critics, Roberto Oliveira Campos, former Minister of Planning and architect of Brazil's "economic miracle," who cites the dual goal of the revolution of 1964 as a redistribution of income through increasing the workers' indirect benefits, such as housing, education, health, and economic development of the poorer regions; and the encouragement of savings and investment, which, "in the long run . . . are the only real means for raising the workers' standard of living, by increasing production and productivity." Then, significantly, he adds:

> If it is true that the revolution's social policy ultimately has brought the workers greater economic gains, it is also true that it gives them less psychological satisfaction. . . . Indirect gains, which are more lasting because less inflationary, give the labor unions less a sense of political power and of a real voice in decisions. . . . Hence the importance of giving the unions broader and more effective functions than only salary ultimatums. . . .[46]

He then goes on to recommend that unions be entrusted with such tasks as the administration of housing cooperatives, educational programs, and the administration of social assistance.

This criticism of the government and the labor unions made by Minister Campos had already been leveled by the ACO in the document cited above. The ACO lamented the fact that the Brazilian labor unions did not assume "the task of the development of the Northeast" and that "the majority of

[43]Ibid.

[44]Neale J. Pearson calls SORPE "perhaps the most successful Brazilian Church effort among rural workers outside of Rio Grande do Norte"; in "Latin American Peasant Pressure Groups and the Modernization Process," *Journal of International Affairs*, Vol. XX, No. 2, 1968.

[45]Helder Câmara, *Terzo Mondo Defraudato* (Milan: EMI, 1968), p. 114.

[46]*Visión* (Mexico City), February 27, 1971, in LADOC, September 1971.

the labor unions . . . contented themselves with discussing questions of salaries," when many other pressing problems were calling for attention.[47]

Dom Helder accuses the government of repressing union activity and persecuting workers who do no more than demand their lawful rights of belonging to a union, earning an adequate wage, enjoying job security, and receiving a pension. Moreover, he charges the government with attempting to prevent the unions from carrying on "the holy and urgent work of conscientization," which he regards as an important and legitimate union function.[48]

A different approach to union activity is that of Fr. Antonio Melo, pastor of Cabo, a town which lies in the midst of a decadent sugar industry on the outskirts of Recife. Fr. Melo has been associated with the Serviço de Assistência Rural in Natal, Rio Grande do Norte, founded by the late Archbishop of Rio de Janeiro, Dom Eugenio Araujo Sales, whose goals were to unionize and make literate the rural people of the Northeast. In a short time Fr. Melo had developed into an able union organizer and the *senhores dos engenhos* (sugar plantation owners) and the *usinas* (sugar mills) felt threatened by the meetings that took place in his rectory. His rural union became so strong that the leftist governor of Pernambuco, according to Fr. Melo, tried to discredit him by showing that the Brazilian Institute for Democratic Action (IBAD), a rightwing organization opposed to the field hands, "was working in my rectory and that I was paid by the Institute."[49]

Since he believed that the Brazilian unions had lost their freedom after the 1964 coup, Dom Helder, having become Archbishop of Recife, decided that any further work in them by the priests was useless. Dom Eugenio, on the other hand, encouraged the priests to continue their union activities. From 1964 on, Fr. Melo's union called four strikes, each terminating, without arrests, in the recognition of the rights of the peasants. In 1966, during a particularly severe economic depression, the *senhores dos engenhos*, who had not been paid by the *usinas*, were unable to pay the workers. Fr. Melo's union called a strike to dramatize to the government the region's plight. Within a few days the authorities and the employers met the workers' demands.

The following year a conflict arose over the local peasants' resentment that the agencies in charge of the development of the Northeast seemed to be according preferential treatment in land redistribution to more qualified outsiders, rather than assisting the local people. Fr. Melo attacked the Brazilian

[47]Helder Câmara, *Terzo Mondo Defraudato*, pp. 23-24.

[48]Helder Câmara, *Rivoluzione nella Pace* (Milan: Jaca Book, 1969) pp. 118-19.

[49]Antonio Callado, *Tempo de Arraes. Padres e Comunistas na Revolução sem Violencia* (Rio de Janeiro: Ed. José Alvaro, 1965), p. 50; and Eloy Dutra, *IBAD Sigla de Corrupção* (Rio de Janeiro: Ed. Civ. Brasileira, 1963), pp. 19, 27, 31, 56, 61.

Institute of Agrarian Reform (IBRA) and the National Institute of Agrarian Development (INDA) for their incompetence and because their programs were causing job displacement. He urged direct action:

> The only advice that I can give to those unemployed and marginalized by the process of regional development, through the fault of the agencies responsible for distributing the land, is to invade the buildings and seats of distribution. . . . When the hour comes to do everything with force . . . I will be at their side. . . . Then everyone will protest, but it will have been they who chose the way of violence.[50]

In 1969 Fr. Melo urgently needed additional land for his pilot program of agrarian reform in Cabo. Over seven hundred families had already been located on a minimum of twenty-five acres each; to distribute less than this amount per family, Fr. Melo claimed, would encourage uneconomical property holdings. Getting no response from the local agencies, he went over their heads and successfully took his case to the authorities in Brasilia.

In 1971 Fr. Melo recorded two additional victories. For years he had been fighting to prevent a group of families from being evicted from 125 acres of land in Camela. The owners, after protracted negotiations, had promised to let the squatters have the land, but when the time came the land had been sold, and the new owner renewed the eviction process. While the federal authorities were favorable, the local authorities and owners remained intransigent. Finally, on September 2, 1971, the *Diario Oficial* published the decree of the Governor of Pernambuco by which the land was expropriated and assigned to the farmers.

The other victory concerned a public housing project. Dom Helder had justifiably attacked this government project on the grounds that the houses' cost exceeded the intended residents' ability to pay. Fr. Melo also criticized the project, but he advised the peasants to sign the contracts, take possession of the houses, and then refuse payment. The ploy succeeded and President Medici ordered the price reduced.

Relations between Fr. Melo and Dom Helder are good, but not enthusiastic. Apparently Dom Helder and his people consider Fr. Melo not sufficiently radical, not sufficiently concerned with structural reform and too trade-unionist. "They accuse me," Fr. Melo has said, "of being a reactionary and playing up to the establishment. . . . It is a fact that I don't take part in any ecclesiastical commissions for the study of social questions. I am too realistic. Papers and academic discussions make me nervous. A *campones* (peasant) doesn't live by slogans. . . ."[51]

---

[50]*Journal do Brasil* (Rio de Janeiro), October 29, 1967. Philippe C. Schmitter traces the history of the Rural Workers' Statute (1963), which permitted unionization of rural workers, and Fr. Melo's efforts to secure compliance with it, in *Interest Conflict and Political Change in Brazil* (Stanford, California: Stanford University Press, 1971) pp. 211-12.

[51]Floridi interview with Fr. Melo, September 13, 1971.

The influence of Marxist ideas has transformed the Brazilian Catholic labor apostolate from reformist to radical. The instrument of radicalization has been *conscientização*, a teaching technique used to stimulate a coming to grips with political and socioeconomic reality.

The Catholic workers' movement in Brazil was embodied chiefly in the *círculos operários* (workers' circles) and the JOC (Young Catholic Workers Movement). The goals of the *círculos*—which were founded in 1932 and by 1962 numbered 375 and had 415,000 members—was "to establish a Christian social order of peace and harmony between capital and labor." Their program included professional and spiritual training, support of the workers' demands, cooperation with the unions to improve the condition of the workers, training labor leaders, and combating extremist ideologies. In a pastoral letter entitled *The Church and Labor,* the Archbishop of Rio de Janeiro, Dom Jaime de Barros Câmara, commended the *círculos'* schools for eliminating adult illiteracy and fighting communism in the union movement.[52]

Today, however, the *círculos* (renamed the Confederação Brasileira de Trabalhadores Cristãos—CBTC) are going through a period of crisis. Interest among both the leaders and the rank and file is flagging, the *círculos* suffer from a conservative and paternalistic image, and there is rivalry and competition with both the unions and the reformist and revolutionary Catholic peasant leagues.[53] As Howard J. Wiarda has written in his detailed examination of the Brazilian Catholic labor movement, the 1964 revolution provoked a crisis within the *círculo* movement. It demonstrated to the Church and to Catholic labor leaders the weakness of the movement's organizational structure and the ineffectiveness and irrelevancy of its program and ideology, and led to an effort to re-examine and revitalize the movement.[54]

The rapid transformation of the Brazilian JOC was due in part to its relationship with the leaders of the European JOC, but mainly to its participation in a literacy drive, which was intended to be a *conscientização* of the masses of workers and peasants. This type of literacy campaign differs fundamentally from that conducted by the *círculos operários* or by other Catholic associations, which are modeled on the Acción Cultural Popular (ACPO) of Colom-

---

[52] Dom Jaime de Barros Câmara, *A Igreja e os Operários, 33a. Carta Pastoral* (Rio de Janeiro: Ed. S. Pio X, 1962). The JOC was introduced in Brazil in 1948 "to evangelize the working youth." In his letter the Cardinal praised the JOC's opposition to compromise with Marxism: "the JOC is giving the country and the Church truly Christian leaders, not affected by Marxist influence. . . ." Only two years later, however, the situation had completely changed, and the JOC, unlike the *círculos operários,* announced their support of the Goulart regime.

[53] Confederação Brasileira de Trabalhadores Cristãos, X Congreso Nacional Circulista (July 15-19, 1970), *Documentos* (Belo Horizonte, Brazil, 1970), pp. 21-22.

[54] Howard J. Wiarda, *The Brazilian Catholic Labor Movement: The Dilemmas of National Development* (Amherst, Massachusetts: Labor Relations and Research Center, University of Massachusetts, 1969), p. 27.

bia, founded in 1947 by Monsignor José Joaquín Salcedo. The ideology of the ACPO is reformist; it seeks to "elevate the peasant on the moral, intellectual and technical level so that he will be able to take his own economic and political decisions, without our indoctrinating him and telling him to rebel."[55]

Conscientização, devised by the Brazilian educator Paulo Freire, is a technique for the achievement of popular liberation through literacy. "Conscientization," says Freire, "implies a historical commitment to make changes." It is predicated on the belief "that when I realize that I am oppressed, I also know I can liberate myself if I transform the concrete situation where I find myself oppressed."[56]

A few years prior to the 1964 Brazilian revolution the Auxiliary Bishop of Natal in northeast Brazil, Dom Eugenio Araujo Sales, launched a literacy drive, the Movement for Basic Education (MEB).[57] In addition to the goal of adult literacy, it was further hoped that the MEB would help to neutralize the appeal of the revolutionary propaganda of the Peasants' League of Francisco Julião and buttress the newly created cooperatives and rural Catholic trade unions. Chiefly for economic reason, the MEB adopted Freire's *conscientização* technique, not perceiving the consequences for its own goals of such a decision.

As a technique for achieving literacy, the Freire method is very successful. In the case of the MEB, before commencing the actual instruction, observers were sent into the field to study the local customs, type of work, interests, and most frequently used vocabulary of the target group. Having discovered these key words, Freire and his collaborators composed texts illustrated by slides. Within a few weeks formerly illiterate adults were reading the core words and constructing phrases. In many instances, these materials had a definite political bias, and two of the pamphlets* were declared subversive and confiscated in February 1964 by order of the then Governor of Guanabara, Carlos Lacerda.

---

[55]*L'Osservatore Romano,* August 25, 1968.

[56]Speech by Paulo Freire, Rome, 1970, in *Contacto* (Mexico City), March 1971 and LADOC, April 1972. See also Paulo Freire, *Pedagogy of the Oppressed* (New York: Herder and Herder, 1970), in which Freire has somewhat modified his views. He criticizes the uncompromising positions of both the rightists who favor the preservation of the status quo and the leftists who believe that utopia will automatically arrive with the overthrow of the existing system. He now stresses the necessity of a period of unified reflection and action in order to achieve liberation of all people. Freire left Brazil in 1964 and is currently on the staff of the World Council of Churches in Geneva, planning an educational program for the Third World.

[57]"Le Mouvement de Natal," in *Perspectives de Catholicité* (Paris), 1964, No. 1, pp. 33-38; see also Marina Bandeira, "Brazil's Basic Educational Movement," in John J. Considine, *The Church in the New Latin America* (Notre Dame, Indiana: Fides Publishers, 1964), pp. 74-82; and Charles Antoine, *Church and Power in Brazil* (Maryknoll, N.Y.: Orbis Books, 1973), pp. 39-45.

*See Appendix, p. 92.

It is significant that many of the MEB instructors were volunteers from Catholic Action and from the Rural Catholic Youth (JAC) and JOC. Another group that adopted the Freire Method was the Ação Popular (AP). This movement, too, was formed by students from Catholic Action; but, contrary to MEB, it was autonomous, independent of the bishops' control, and, although it had priest advisers, it explicitly excluded priests from membership. The AP had by then become quite radical, and was working with the Communists in student and agrarian worker organizations. The AP supported the Peasants' League of Francisco Julião rather than the rural Catholic unions and endorsed strikes and land seizures. Under the aegis of the AP, politicization ultimately prevailed over conscientization in the MEB.

The Brazilian JOC has moved far from its original aims. In a 1967 manifesto it seeks to arouse the sleeping consciences of the workers in order that they may embark on the struggle "for the liberation of the working class." The manifesto confronts the hierarchy with a series of demands, including one "that paternalism and assistance (such as handouts of food, medicine, and clothing), which anesthetize the poor and leave the consciences of the rich more tranquil, be completely eliminated."[58]

In the wake of the 1964 coup all rivals of the *círculos* were purged or liquidated. The conservative leaders of the *círculos,* according to Wiarda, collaborated with the new military regime, and thereby regained their unchallenged claim to leadership of the Catholic social movement. However, this cooperation with the military junta caused the CBTC to be expelled from CLAT, to which it was affiliated prior the 1964 coup, and fragmented the movement between the old-line conservatives and the liberals who believe it must open itself to the ideas of the Brazilian Catholic Left. At the present time there is "a great deal of intellectual ferment going on within the movement to devise a new set of aims and objectives that will make it more relevant to the radically changed Brazilian social context. The question of exactly how to do this has not yet been answered."[59]

COSTA RICA

Protest songs, poems, slides, and posters are popular communications media among the practitioners of *conscientização*. One evening during the May 1971 meeting of the CELAM bishops in San José, Costa Rica, a group of Catholic youths, protesting "all the irregularities daily perpetrated by the

---

[58]*Vozes* (Petropolis, Brazil), October 1967, pp. 879ff.
[59]Wiarda, *op. cit.,* pp. 27 and 42.

Catholic Church in Costa Rica, against all recommendations of Medellín,"
sang:

> What will the Holy Father who lives in Rome say
> About the killing of his dove.
> Look how [the bishops] preach tranquility
> While in reality they take it away from us.
> Look how they speak of freedom
> While in reality they take it away from us.
> Look how enthusiastically they pass sentences
> Knowing that they are killing the innocent.[60]

Another song, "If Christ Could See Them," accuses the Archbishop of San José of avoiding communication with the common people; of living in "three castles"; of owning ten automobiles; of wearing silks and diamonds while the people are dirty and in rags; of removing from their parishes good priests, "real human beings, respected and full of compassion"; and of rewarding with honors and emoluments those who practice usury and greed.[61]

The Costa Rican clergy includes priests of international repute who serve the poor and the workers, such as Fr. Benjamin Nuñez, founder of the Confederación Costarricense del Trabajo Rerum Novarum (CCT). Soon after its inception in 1943, the CCT had fifteen union affiliates. Its strength was chiefly among the workers of the coffee plantations, railroads, and San José factories.[62] According to Victor Alba, "the CCT member unions never questioned the religious affiliations of their members." In the words of Fr. Nuñez: "What we consider fundamental are the individual human being and his sense of dignity. As a result, we are neither Communists nor Socialists, but, if I may be allowed to coin the term, 'personists.'"[63]

The chief rival of the CCT was the Communist Confederación de Trabajadores de Costa Rica (CTCR, now the Confederación General de Trabajadores Costarricenses—CGTC). The focal point of the struggle between the two federations was the banana-growing regions, which had traditionally been dominated by the Communist unions. In the late 1950's, the CGTC became the largest single labor central in the country.[64]

Today the Costa Rican Christian labor federation no longer bears the name "Rerum Novarum," after the famous encyclical of Pope Leo XIII, and no

---

[60]*La Repı blica* (San José, Costa Rica), May 12, 1971.

[61]The priests referred to in the song, Frs. Muñoz and Solís, during Holy Week had organized a Via Crucis of protest, using texts of Che Guevara, Camilo Torres, and the Costa Rican Marxist poet, Jorge de Bravo. Liturgies of this kind were also held in Brazil and other Latin American countries. The bishops said they disciplined the priests not because of the liturgies' social content, but because they deviated from the approved Catholic ceremonial. See Alexis U. Floridi, *Radicalismo Cattolico Brasiliano* (Rome: Instituto Editoriale del Mediterraneo, 1968), p. 21.

[62]Robert J. Alexander, *Organized Labor in Latin America* (New York: The Free Press, 1965), p. 216.

[63]Victor Alba, *op. cit.*, pp. 279-80.

[64]Alexander, *Organized Labor in Latin America*, p. 216.

longer endorses the anticommunism of Fr. Nuñez. Today it is called the Confederación de Obreros y Campesinos Cristianos (COCC), and it is affiliated with CLAT through the Confederación Centroamericana de Trabajadores. According to the Secretary General of the COCC, Alcimiro Herrera Torres, the doctrine of the Church has evolved since the times of Leo XIII and Fr. Nuñez, and the workers, in order to be victorious, must unite even with the Communists of the CGTC: "This year, for the first time," the approving Secretary General said, "the workers of Costa Rica celebrated May Day together." Unfortunately, he added, after the celebration the ORIT-affiliated Confederación Costarricense de Trabajadores Democráticos (CCTD) returned to its unshakable anticommunist position, thus rupturing the workers' united front.[65]

A Catholic-Communist alliance is also advocated by the Communist People's Vanguard Party of Costa Rica (PVPCR):

> The tasks of the anti-imperialist, agrarian and democratic revolution, and in the future the tasks of socialism, will be carried out only on the basis of joint action by the majority of people. No single party or group is capable of establishing revolutionary power single-handed. . . . Our party shall strive to create a united front . . . of Catholics and other religious groups adhering to the revolutionary process.[66]

The PVPCR appeals particularly to the banana and other farm workers:

> Agricultural workers constitute an important segment of the working class. For a historically long period of time agricultural workers at banana plantations played a leading role in demonstrations of the proletariat. . . .[67]

During the meeting of the CELAM bishops and the congress of the PVPCR, held almost concurrently in May 1971 in San José, there was agitation for a strike by the banana workers. However, despite the united pro-strike actions of the Communist and Catholic unions, the workers voted not to strike.[68]

MESSAGE TO THE PEOPLE OF THE THIRD WORLD

The most concise statement of Dom Helder Câmara's philosophy is his attempt to convey the meaning of the encyclical *Populorum Progressio* (The Development of Peoples) of Pope Paul VI in the phrase "today Christianity is the economic development of mankind."[69]

---

[65] Floridi interview with Alcimiro Herrera Torres, San José, Costa Rica, May 11, 1971; see also *CCT en Acción, Órgano Oficial de Información y Orientación de la Confederación Centroamericana de Trabajadores* (San José, Costa Rico), No. 6, November-December 1970, p. 4.
[66] *Information Bulletin, World Marxist Review* publishers, 1971, No. 12-13, pp. 88-94.
[67] *Ibid.*
[68] *La República* (San José, Costa Rica), May 15, 1971.
[69] See *La Vie Catholique Illustrée,* September 21-27, 1966, pp. 11-14; see also Carlo Fiore, "Da Recife un Grido dall'Allarme," in *Dimensioni* (Italy), 1968, No. 3, p. 25.

This view is elaborated in the *Message to the People of the Third World** (1967), inspired by Dom Helder and signed by bishops from Brazil, Colombia, Algeria, Egypt, Lebanon, Yugoslavia, China, Oceania, and Laos. The authors of this document, "seeing the movements that are stirring up the peasant and worker masses of the Third World today," address themselves to the priests, laity, and "all men of goodwill" in the Third World, in order to "give courage to all who suffer and strive for justice, that indispensable condition of peace." According to these bishops, the gospel defends the necessity of radical revolution, touching all aspects of life, "physical and social as well as spiritual and personal." Yet at times the Church has erroneously allowed itself to become too closely identified with a particular ephemeral system of government—in this case, capitalism—which, say the bishops, is not consonant with the teachings of the gospel:

> The moment a system fails to provide for the common good and shows favoritism to a particular few, the Church has the duty not only to denounce the injustice, but also to cut free from that unjust system, seeking to collaborate with some other system more just and likely to meet the necessity of the times.[70]

Are these Third World bishops merely opportunistically seeking to align the Church with the revolution they feel is inevitable? On this subject Dom Helder has written:

> With us, without us, or perhaps despite us, the masses are going to wake up. Woe to Christianity if tomorrow the awakened masses feel convinced that their religion, out of fear of governments and the mighty of the earth, abandoned them. . . .[71]

Of course, the bishops affirm, "not every revolution is necessarily good. . . . Atheism and collectivism, which certain movements pick up as they grow, are serious dangers for humanity."

However, "the Church can only rejoice as she sees another social system arising which is less alien" to the moral values of the gospel, solidarity and fraternity:

> Rather than shun this, let us welcome it with joy, as a social way of life more in harmony with our times and with the gospels. Thus we can keep people from associating God and religion with those forces of oppression that grind down the workers and the poor—feudalism, capitalism and imperialism.[72]

---

[70]*Catholic Mind*, January 1968, in LADOC, July 1970; and René Laurentin, *Flashes sull'America Latina* (Rome: Ediz. Paoline, 1970), pp. 99ff.

[71]Paulo R. Schilling, *Helder Câmara*, excerpts in LADOC, October 1970; see also Helder Câmara, "Los Pecados del Mundo," in *Una Respuesta al Clamor de los Pobres* (Nueve de Julio, Argentina: Ed. Busqueda, 1968), pp. 52-53.

[72]LADOC, July 1970.

*See Appendix, pp. 96-98.

In the view of the signatories of the *Message to the People of the Third World*, the abuses of "totalitarian collectivism and religious persecution" have ensued from these oppressions which they condemn. Therefore,

> the Church salutes with pride and joy a new humanity in which honor is conferred not on the money accumulated in the hands of a few, but on workers, laborers, and farmers.[73]

Addressing themselves more directly to the rights of workers in the penultimate section of the document, the bishops assert that "within each nation, workers have the right and the duty to join in real unions in order to demand and protect their rights." The rights they enumerate are a fair salary, paid sick leave, social security, housing, and participation in management. Merely having laws to this effect on the books does not suffice; governments must ensure their enforcement. And they appeal to governments to put an end to the "class warfare" waged by the wealthy against the workers in the form of low wages and intolerable working conditions.

The signatories of the *Message to the People of the Third World*, like other spokesmen of the Latin American Catholic Left, have been attracted to the Yugoslavian system of decentralizing managerial responsibility as a model for Latin America. In a section on "the dignity of man and his labor" they indicate agreement with the Bishop of Split, Yugoslavia, who stated:

> If the workers cannot become in some way owners of their work, all our reforming of structures will be futile. Even if workers get a raise in salary occasionally in a given economic system, they will not be satisfied. They want to be the owners, not the sellers, of their work.

PERU

The Yugoslavian model of worker self-management does not hold universal appeal among the Latin American Catholic Left. When a similar arrangement was instituted in Peru in 1970 by the government of General Juan Velasco Alvarado, the priests of ONIS (National Office of Social Information), a group of about one hundred missionaries who work with Peruvian priests, opposed it.[74]

Under the Peruvian General Law of Industries, workers become shareholders in their companies, until, over a period of time, they eventually own 50 percent of the business.

---

[73]*Ibid.*

[74]See *Time Magazine*, February 22, 1971. The question of Yugoslavian self-management was posed to Fidel Castro by Catholic youths during his visit to Chile in December 1971. Castro dismissed worker self-management as another bourgeois scheme which would artificially create a privileged class of factory workers above the rest of the labor force.

The Catholic hierarchy of Peru welcomed the innovation. The Bishop of the *pueblos jóvenes* (young towns) in Lima's slums, Luis Bambaren, S.J., pronounced the law "fully in harmony with Christian social teaching." The Law of Industries, he added, "in its search for integral development, promotes true social justice. I would hope that all of us Peruvians would grasp the significance of this moment and our duty to participate in the building of the new society."[75]

A year after the enactment of the Law of Industries, President Velasco for the first time described the Peruvian revolution as "socialist." But, rejecting the possibility of Marxist socialism, he asserted that the revolution was being carried out by the armed forces

> within the most illustrious tradition of libertarian, socialist and humanist thinking. . . . In this way a 'reformed' private industry, alongside cooperatives and state enterprises, would be organized in such a way that all classes would be pulling together for the common good, instead of struggling against each other to the detriment of society.[76]

The Peruvian press has pointed out the similarities between the "industrial community" and the Yugoslavian model. *El Comercio* of Lima questioned the wisdom of adopting "imported models" at a time when indigenous solutions to Peru's problems are being emphasized, and suggested that Peruvian technical experts should have studied the success or failure of these policies elsewhere.[77]

Sociologist Carlos Delgado, adviser to the Peruvian military government, has praised the idea of the labor community as a bridge between social classes. He denied any Yugoslav influence on the regime, observing that "we are trying to emerge from the capitalist mold without falling into communism, while the Yugoslavs are trying to emerge from the Communist mold without falling into capitalism."[78]

Because the General Law of Industries does not abolish private ownership of the means of production and seeks harmony between capital and labor, the priests of ONIS reject it as merely another form of neocapitalism:

> the General Law of Industries does not usher in the day of social ownership of the means of production. Rather it seems to promote a neocapitalistic sort of society in which (a) after a passing nod to

---

[75]*Noticias Aliadas* (Peruvian Catholic News Agency), August 1, 1970, and LADOC, November 1970.
[76]*Latin America* (London weekly), August 6, 1971. In September 1973 the Peruvian military government introduced plans for further economic innovation, in the form of collectively-owned, worker-managed enterprises which will comprise a new and ultimately dominant economic sector, called *propiedad social* or social property.
[77]*El Comercio* (Lima), December 16, 1971.
[78]*Latin America* (London), August 6, 1971.

social ownership, private ownership is further spread, and (b) efforts are made to speed up industrial development by tightening state controls and enlarging the extent of state ownership in industries.[79]

ONIS also opposes the land reform enacted by the Peruvian military government for the same reasons: it perpetuates capitalism by preserving property rights in the distribution of shares to the peasant.[80]

While the priests of ONIS make no mention of the implication of the industrial community for the rights of unions, Julio Cruzado, Secretary General of the Central de Trabajadores del Peru (CTP), the labor arm of APRA, registered labor's misgivings about this feature of the new system.* Although he acknowledged that certain advantages do accrue to the workers, he emphasized that such gains must not be at the expense of union rights:

> the union has the task of protecting the interests of the workers . . . . however much community may exist in Peru, our unions will never disappear. The unions must become the instrument that assists both this communitary interest of the workers and our own effort, because both offer permanent guarantees for the communitary development of Peru.[81]

The priests of ONIS stage mass street demonstrations in the name of the "proletariat" aimed at the liberation of the oppressed through the establishment of socialism. They appear to give higher priority to promoting "an autonomous popular mobilization and cultural revolution" than to working to achieve the concrete demands of the unions. In the case of the 1971 teachers' strike, for example, they offered their services as mediators, but did not take to the streets in a show of solidarity with the striking teachers.[82]

An incident indirectly involving ONIS that occurred in conjunction with the May 1971 CELAM conference in San José, Costa Rica, points up how ONIS exemplifies one of the most perplexing dilemmas for Latin American Catholicism: the necessity of relying on foreign priests to help fill the gap in the ratio of priests-to-laymen, and the consequent importation of ideologies that have their roots in other sociopolitical milieus.

---

[79]*Expreso* (Lima), August 17, 1970, in LADOC, November 1970.

[80] *Time Magazine,* February 22, 1971.

[81]Julio Cruzado Zavala, *Los Trabajadores y la Problemática Nacional* (Lima, Peru: CTP, 1971). On October 13, 1970, the Peruvian military government under President Velasco adopted a measure directed at enforcing penalties against parties who attempt to resolve industrial disputes by illegal means. The measure, designed to curb the labor strife resulting from a series of illegal strikes by Communist-led unions, which claimed credit for winning wage increases and improved working conditions, was applauded by the CTP, and attacked as a threat to the working class by the Communist Confederación General de Trabajadores del Peru (CGTP) and by the Marxist Federación de Empleados Bancarios (FEB). U.S. Department of Labor, Bureau of Labor Statistics, *Labor Developments Abroad,* March 1971.

[82]*La Razón* (Buenos Aires), September 16, 1971.

*See Appendix, pp. 95-96.

Just prior to the CELAM conference a bloody fracas erupted between the police and squatters who had illegally seized some land in Pamplona, outside the Peruvian capital; one man was killed and sixty wounded, mostly policemen. The Peruvian press attributed the disturbance to an attempt to discredit the Peruvian military government during the meeting of the governors of the Interamerican Development Bank.[83] A priest from the United States, Fr. Carmelo G. Lamazza, organized a "protest liturgy" in which he invited the residents of nearby parishes to participate. Believing this action provocative, Bishop Bambaren at first asked Lamazza to abandon the project, and then, seeing that this was impossible, volunteered to preside over the liturgy to ensure that it would not degenerate into an anti-government demonstration. But, "possibly due to an outbreak of emotional feelings on my part," as he later observed,[84] his words were misconstrued, and the Bishop was arrested. The arrest of Bishop Bambaren lasted only a few hours and the affair ended with mutual apologies and the resignation of the Peruvian Minister of the Interior. But the incident dramatized how sensitive situations can be exacerbated by the involvement of foreign priests.

Because the Catholic Church in Latin America does not have sufficient indigenous clergy, their numbers must be supplemented by foreign priests. Recognizing this need, Pope John XXIII formally requested during the 1960's that religious orders in the United States send 10 per cent of their priests to Latin America. Mutchler attributes the massive influx of North American, French, Belgian, and West German priests into Latin America in the 1960's to the threat of "another Cuba." He places such significance on the importation of foreign priests that he states that "the Cuban revolution may be seen as the decisive event in the development of Latin Catholicism in the 1960's."[85]

The presence of these priests has been interpreted in two opposing ways: as the symbol of "spiritual imperalism,"[86] or as a dangerous reinforcement of local agitators. Bishop Eduardo Pironio, Secretary General of CELAM, characterized the problem as follows:

> A superficial knowledge of Latin America—and of the special vocation of our Church—could lead the apostolic personnel who come here so generously from overseas to a serious misconception: an exclusively socioeconomic notion of the Church's role; it could give

[83]*Expreso* (Lima), May 13, 1971.
[84]*Pamplona: Más allá de los Hechos* (Lima, Peru: CEP, May 1971, mimeo.), p. 21.
[85]David E. Mutchler, *The Church as a Political Factor in Latin America* (New York: Frederick A. Praeger, 1971), p. 63.
[86]Ivan Illich, "The Seamy Side of Charity," *America* (New York), January 21, 1967. Illich, who left the priesthood in 1968, founded a training center in Cuernavaca, Mexico, for people planning to work in Latin America. In 1969 the Holy See forbade priests and nuns to study there, although some continue to do so.

them an excessive eagerness for a political commitment and a fascination with revolution and violence, either because they don't really see those goals in proper focus, or because they are determined to pursue them outside the framework of their churchly functions.[87]

Fr. Lamazza did not follow the CELAM guidelines nor the advice of his superiors, yet in the official communiqué of the archbishopric of Lima on the incident at Pamplona his actions were fully condoned and defended. Two other foreign priests, Fr. Eugenio Bourbon and Fr. José Luis Gómez Morales, were expelled from Peru in February 1972 for participating in political demonstrations; ONIS immediately defended them and called for their return to Peru.[88]

The priests of ONIS part company with anyone who supports the Peruvian military regime as a first step toward genuine socialism. One leftist who did so was Hector Bejar, a Peruvian guerrilla leader, who, after being released from prison by President Velasco in 1970, stated:

> To the workers and students who believe in the guerrillas as a hope for the salvation of Peru, I must tell them . . . that I do support this process, and not because of opportunism or any sinecure. I support it because it is a stage of transformation, which, in order to reach culmination, requires the participation of the people and of all the revolutionaries, because a revolution can begin without the people, but it cannot fully culminate without them.[89]

Reviewing the Pamplona incident, the Lima newspaper *Expreso* commented that it "demonstrates that the ONIS priests do not miss an opportunity to protest against Peruvian 'neo-capitalism' and to support revolution."[90] They have no confidence in the reforms of the military regime, the paper continued, because the industrial community is not intended to be an instrument of the

---

[87]*Priests and Religious for Latin America*. Proceedings and Conclusions of the First Inter-American Conference of Major Superiors. Mexico City, February 8-12, 1971 (Washington, D.C.: USCC, Division for Latin America, 1971). Bishop Pironio made these statements while addressing the delegates of the General Council of the Commission for Latin America (COGECAL), in Rome, September 29, 1971.

[88]According to another version of the Pamplona incident which circulated in Lima, Bishop Bambaren and the Minister of the Interior, General Artola, were born in the same town, and their relationship had become rather strained. At Christmas 1970, the General had distributed some Christmas cakes in order to increase his popularity. In a sermon the Bishop alluded to this act, saying that the poor cannot be helped by small gifts, but only by structural changes of society. The General, according to this version, did not forget the offense, and at the first opportunity took revenge. Another version goes so far as to claim that General Artola had surreptitiously tried, with the help of the right, to provoke an incident with the Catholic hierarchy in order to oust President Velasco. See *Los Repartos de Navidad. Parroquia San Cristobal, Comunidad Cristiana de Tres Compuertas, 1970* (Lima: CEP, 1971), pp. 11-12.

[89]*Intercontinental Press*, May 24, 1971; on Hector Bejar and other Peruvian guerrillas see Guillermo Lobaton, *Secondo Fronte. Teoria della Guerriglia e Appello alla Lotta Armata negli Scritti del Capo dei Tupac Amaru* (Milan: Feltrinelli, 1970), pp. 53ff.

[90]July 14, 1972. On the Peruvian military see Edwin Lieuwen, "The Changing Role of the Armed Forces," in Robert D. Tomasek, *Latin American Politics* (Garden City, N.Y.: Doubleday & Company, 1966), pp. 57-84.

class struggle, and because they do not accept its revolutionary nature. They believe the concept of the industrial community is a subterfuge, a sop to the workers to divert them from fulfilling their true revolutionary mission. Ideologically they are close to the Chilean priests of the Movement of Christians for Socialism and MAPU in rejecting both Christian Democracy, which cuts across class lines, and the non-Marxist "Christian socialism" of the Christian Left. Both groups believe that there can be no "Christian humanism" apart from "Marxist humanism," and that "the philosophical divisions between Christians and Marxists become secondary when faced with the urgency of an effective revolutionary action."[91]

---

[91]¿*Una Izquierda Cristiana?* (Lima, Peru: CEP, 1971), p. 46, and *Cristianos por el Socialismo. Primer Encuentro Latinoamericano* (Lima, Peru: CEP, 1972) p. 29. The MAPU and the Christian Left were the result of two divisions which occurred in the Chilean Christian Democratic party in 1969 and in 1971. Both were represented in President Allende's Popular Unity (UP) government.

III

BEYOND THE CHURCH'S AND WORKERS' AIMS

The choice of socialism as the only path to liberation by some progressive Latin American clergymen sometimes leads them to support guerrilla violence, subversion, or dictatorship. The claimed "national," "humanist" and "Christian" content of this socialism may be submerged in the ideology and tactics of movements, such as Peronism or Castroism, which may entail suppression of the very individual and collective rights these progressive clergymen seek to defend.

In this chapter we examine these revolutionary options of Catholic priests and nuns in Argentina, Chile, Colombia, Bolivia, Guatemala, Uruguay, and Brazil, and discuss the opposition to them of both the Catholic hierarchy, represented by the Latin American Bishops' Conference (CELAM), and the Catholic labor movement.

THE ARGENTINIAN MOVEMENT OF
PRIESTS FOR THE THIRD WORLD (MPTW)

The Message to the People of the Third World, initiated by Dom Helder Câmara, was not generally approved by the Latin American Catholic hierarchy. It was more favorably received by the progressive priests of Argentina, who adopted it as the basis for their social action, and drew from it the conclusions that socialism is necessary for the achievement of Latin American liberation, and subversion and violence may be permissible if they are the only means to achieve it.

According to one of these priests, Fr. Domingo Bresci, the Movement of Priests for the Third World (MPTW) was formed in December 1967 in response to the fact that no Argentinian priest had been among the signatories of the Message to the People of the Third World. A number of Argentinian priests therefore circulated a statement to be signed by their colleagues supporting the document. "The response," notes Fr. Bresci, "was unexpectedly enthusiastic: 270 signatures in the first instance, growing to 400 within a short period of time, revealing a strong current of opinion among the clergy."[1]

The number of priests in the MPTW has remained more or less constant. Their bulletin, *Enlace* (bond, link), consisting of a few mimeographed sheets sent to the members and to "persons closely linked to them because of common activities," has never exceeded five hundred in circulation, out of a total

---

[1] IDOC-International (North American edition), December 12, 1970, pp. 59-61.

Argentinian clergy of over five thousand. But even if they are a minority, the *tercermundista* priests, as they are commonly called, should not be underestimated, because of the volatile political and economic situation of the country and the receptivity to radical ideas of various groups seeking change.

The goals of the MPTW were first set forth in coherent form in the Basic Agreements issued at their second national meeting in Colonia Caroya, Córdoba Province, in May 1969.[2] In this document, the members of the MPTW assert their obligation, "as human beings, Christians, and priests," to

> join in the revolutionary process for *urgent, radical change* of existing structures and to reject formally the capitalistic system we see around us and every kind of economic, political and cultural imperialism.

They pledge to seek a "Latin American brand of socialism":

> This socialism will not necessarily mean following out programs dictated by parties in this or any other part of the world, but it will necessarily mean a socialization of the means of production, of economic and political power, and of culture.

In a subsequent document, entitled *Our Commitment to Liberation,* issued at the conclusion of their third national meeting, the priests of the MPTW added several important precisions to their endorsement of socialism, especially in the Argentine context:

> The revolutionary process and the tendency toward socialism are not something just beginning today. In Argentina, for example, our experience under Perón—and the lasting fidelity of the masses to the Peronist movement—were significant steps in our people's incorporation into the revolutionary process. The scattered revolutionary forces must be made aware of this trend; in that way all who yearn for national liberation will join in a common cause.[3]

The irony of this statement will not be lost on those who recall that in 1955 it was the politically active priests who opposed Perón. Now the situation has come full circle and the priests of the MPTW endorse Peronism as a revolutionary mass movement.

Concerning the "Christian" nature of their organization, the priests of the MPTW made a special point of affirming that their movement "is a sacerdotal, hence a Christian, organization." In fact, they attribute the movement's identification with socialism—"in the sense we give it"—to their judgment that socialism is "more in harmony with the gospel, and one of the principal elements in the 'signs of the times'" (making no distinction in importance between the two).

---

[2]*Esquiú* (Buenos Aires Catholic weekly), September 28, 1969; in LADOC, July 1970.
[3]LADOC, July 1970. See also special report, "Who are the Priests of the Third World?" *Jerónimo* (Buenos Aires), August 1970; in LADOC, December 1970.

The MPTW priests abjure any political vocation:

> for a variety of reasons, our movement is not, does not wish to be, and cannot be, a political party. For the same reasons, it refuses to become a revolutionary cabal that would seize political power.[4]

It pledges to respect the freedom of choice of other organizations' tactics, strategies, and policies, while nevertheless remaining "convinced that authentic socialism will come to Latin America only when real revolutionaries, who come from the people and remain true to the people, seize power."

On the question of violence, the priests of the MPTW expressed their position in a statement sent to the Second General Assembly of the Latin American bishops at Medellín (August 1968). In it they affirmed the necessity:

1. of avoiding by all means the . . . confusion of the unjust violence of those who maintain a system of oppression and the just violence of the oppressed, who see themselves obliged to resort to it in order to find liberation;
2. of proclaiming the right of these peoples to their legitimate defense;
3. of assuring Christians a wide range of freedom in the choice of means they consider most suitable for achieving this liberation and constructing this society. . . . It is not a question of making violence an ideal, but of giving a new dimension to the right, so often recognized in theory, of any oppressed community to react, even violently, against an unjust aggressor. . . .[5]

It is quite possible that the loose structure of the MPTW, which precludes the attribution of statements or actions of individual members to the movement as a whole, is an intentional device by which it hoped to escape the control and censure of the Church. In this vein, Bishop Devoto of Goya, one of the few Argentinian bishops to show some sympathy for the movement, gave the MPTW priests the following counsel:

> I take the liberty of advising you not to give in to the temptation of organizing yourselves. I think there are some who would take great interest in seeing you 'organized.' Know how to preserve the freshness and suppleness of a Movement which, rather than by dictating 'norms,' gives a spirit to those who like to feel engaged as a Church.[6]

Bishop Devoto was evidently also trying to curtail the political involvement of the MPTW priests, fearing that such involvement would be detrimental to their prestige as priests.

---

[4]LADOC, July 1970.
[5]IDOC-International, December 12, 1970, p. 74; see also Rolando Concatti and Domingo Bresci, eds., *Sacerdotes para el Tercer Mundo*, 2nd ed. (Buenos Aires: Publicaciones del MSTM, 1970), p. 50.
[6]*Letter to the MPTW Priests*, April 30, 1969, in Concatti and Bresci, *op. cit.* pp. 69-70. According to Church law, it is doubtful, in fact, whether a movement of priests that is completely independent from the hierarchy and pursues goals that are not strictly religious is a lawful movement.

In August 1969 the Archbishop of Corrientes, Francisco Vicentín, polled the priests of his diocese concerning their opinion of the MPTW. The results of the inquiry are reported in the following summation:

> Their activity has about it the aura of aggression and violence; they give the appearance of social agitators; they seem to give absolute priority to the socioeconomic sphere and hence can be taken for Marxists; they concern themselves with matters which the Archbishop would rather they left alone; all this seems a pastoral deformation which threatens to disrupt the Christian community.[7]

The Suffragan Archbishop of Buenos Aires, Juan C. Aramburu, has forbidden the priests to pass resolutions and to organize public demonstrations without prior permission of the Church authorities. However, the MPTW priests have ignored the orders of the archbishops and continued their political activities.

As previously noted, the progressive clergy frequently quote official documents of the popes and bishops as justification for their actions. Throughout Latin America they refer to the Medellín documents, and in Argentina they cite the Declaration of San Miguel (April 1969), the document in which the Argentine bishops apply to their country the decisions of Medellín. In the chapter entitled "Popular Pastoral Work" the Argentine bishops wrote:

> The Church, as an institution distinct from civil society and the temporal order, which have their own autonomy, has the right to judge . . . the life and structure of that society . . . and to denounce wrongful situations.[8]

They go on to say that the Argentinian Church feels called upon to "insert itself and incarnate itself in the national experience of the Argentine people" and that they should themselves strive "to be faithful to our people."

Two MPTW theologians, Lucio Gera and Guillermo Rodríguez Melgarejo, in response to this declaration, ask: "Where is this 'people,' and what does it mean to 'incarnate itself in the people'?" They paraphrase this passage to mean: "The Church must consult the national conscience of the people in order to plot out its mission"; moreover, "the signs of the times are present and legible in the very activities of that people, and in the events that impinge on it." To these two MPTW priests, this chapter of the bishops' document is far more significant than many have perceived:

> In resumé, then, this chapter comes out of nowhere, unannounced, unexpected. No doubt the document understates a bit what it is really saying by its style, which seems to cloak its thought as if it feared being too clear and perhaps being repudiated by those it was meant for. We think it still has not ben read—and certainly not grasped—by many. Otherwise it would have aroused a storm of reactions in agreement or disagreement that so far has not occurred.[9]

---

[7]IDOC-International, December 12, 1970, pp. 84-85.
[8]*Iglesia Latinoamericana: ¿Protesta o Profecía?* (Avellaneda, Argentina: Ed. Busqueda, 1969), pp. 129ff.
[9]*Víspera* (Montevideo), February 1970, in LADOC, December 1970.

52

The publicity accorded the document issued at the conclusion of the second national meeting of the MPTW at Colonia Caroya, Córdoba, in May 1969, elicited a reply by Archbishop Aramburu of Buenos Aires. He argued that "it would be . . . harmful . . . to try to create systematically in the people a feeling of desperation or to make it lose any hope in the solution of its problems. By sowing desperation one can only reap tragic fruits." He condemned the condoning of violence, "by presenting armed uprising as a true and effective solution for social problems," as contrary to both the San Miguel declaration of the Argentine bishops and the conclusions of Medellín. "We cannot invoke the simple establishment of socialism," he concluded, "as a reaction to the mistakes of . . . capitalism."[10]

The debate over whether the priests of the MPTW were condoning violence, exacerbating social tensions, and instilling a sense of desperation in the people, came to a head a few days after the Colonia Caroya meeting, during the Córdoba riots of May 29-30, 1969, which are known as *Cordobazo*. The regional coordinators of the MPTW viewed the burnings and destruction of property as symptoms of the larger social ill:

> It is wrong to say that the burnings and destruction were the result of a premeditated plan or of wanton vandalism. . . . It is wrong to say that what happened was directed by 'alien extremist groups' on behalf of outside interests. . . . We believe that what happened was the spontaneous reaction of a people gradually coming to an awareness of its own dignity. The root of all this . . . is to be found in the situation of oppression and injustice which fully justify it. We maintain that what is at play is not simply revenge but the will of the people to assume the responsibility of directing the destiny of the nation.

They appealed to both the government and the people:

> To those in power we say: put down your arms before it is too late. To the leaders of the people we say: the people must be organized on basic issues. It is essential that objectives be clarified, not simply the immediate objective—struggle against existing structures—but the more distant objective as well—the construction of a new society. It is necessary to reflect in depth, to elaborate in advance the elements of a new order, to awaken everyone to the necessity of beginning to construct now the world of the future.[11]

Some MPTW priests have been linked to guerrilla violence. When Fr. Alberto Carbone, a member of the secretariat of the MPTW and director of its publication, *Enlace,* was arrested on July 8, 1970, for suspicion of complicity in the kidnapping and murder of former President Aramburu, the

---

[10]*AICA* (weekly bulletin of the Agencia Informativa Católica Argentina—Buenos Aires), July 30, 1969, pp. 21-23; Archbishop Aramburu's declaration is dated July 15, 1969.
[11]IDOC-International, December 12, 1970, pp. 73-74; see also Carlos A. Sacheri, *La Iglesia Clandestina* (Buenos Aires: Ed. del Cruzamante, 1970), pp. 114-48.

MPTW affirmed the innocence of the arrested priest, but reiterated its "respect" for the members' decision to resort to violence.[12] The Jesuit magazine *CIAS* attributed the arrest of Fr. Carbone to a slander campaign against the MPTW, but added:

> It is undeniable that certain individuals [of the MPTW] seem to see no alternative, and would probably welcome, counter-violence to match what they deem to be the prevailing institutionalized violence.

The magazine concurred with a statement issued by the national committee of the Christian Family Movement in Argentina which, while praising the MPTW's "obvious pastoral concern," pleaded

> with those priests who have come out as apostles of violence, among whom are some of the Church's finest, to ponder in humble sincerity the probable effect of such preaching, which almost always is purely speculative, on minds that are generous but immature if not sometimes unbalanced.[13]

CIAS regretted that those who "pressured in favor of a violent option beyond the actual conscience of the people" were incurring the "danger of a 'leftist clericalism,'" and urged that "the people" alone should chart their history. Fr. Carbone was also arrested for alleged participation in an attack on a police station in January 1972, and four other priests were charged with belonging to the *Montoneros* (Peronist) guerrillas.

REACTION TO THE MPTW BY THE ARGENTINIAN CATHOLIC WORKERS AND THE CHURCH

Do the priests of the MPTW have popular support, or have they arrogated to themselves the role of propagandists for what are merely their own minority prescriptions?

While generalizations about public opinion in any context can be disputed, the rejection of the philosophy of the MPTW by the organized Catholic workers of the *círculos católicos de obreros*, by representatives of the Argentinian clergy, and by the Permanent Commission of the Argentinian hierarchy is a matter of record.[14]

Bishops and priests have played a role in social and union affairs in Argentina since the beginning of this century, in a far more hostile and anticlerical environment than the present one. The origins of the Catholic workers' move-

---

[12]IDOC-International, December 12, 1970, p. 88.

[13]*CIAS* (Buenos Aires), August-September, 1970, pp. 28-29.

[14]Carlos A. Sacheri, *op. cit.*, pp. 155-70; the author cites (p. 160) thirty-six Argentinian clergymen who signed a statement expressing opposition to the MPTW. See also the report of a debate between a representative of the MPTW, Fr. Vernazza, and Fr. Julio Menvielle, a well-known Argentinian politico-religious writer, in *Esquiú*, April 18 and May 23, 1971; see also the latter's book, *Un Progresismo Vergonzante* (Buenos Aires: Ed. Cruz y Fierro, 1967).

ment date from 1892, the year following the encyclical *Rerum Novarum,* when Fr. Federico Grote founded the first *círculo de obreros.* Among the early achievements of the *círculos* were the Weekly Rest Law (1904), the Working Women and Minors' Law (1907), and the law on the apprenticeship of minors (1944).[15] In 1919 the *círculos* participated in the first Latin American Conference of Catholic Union Movements. In 1930 the name of the movement was changed to Federación de Círculos Católicos de Obreros (Federation of Catholic Workers' Circles). Following the Council Vatican II, the Federation updated its bylaws and guiding principles, which were then republished in 1972 on the occasion of its eightieth anniversary. A review of these principles underscores how much they differ from those of the MPTW.

The Federation of Catholic Workers' Circles supports: (1) an "unbreachable fidelity to democracy, which guarantees the defense of the inalienable rights of man, the family and the worker," without dependence on political parties, and in harmony and solidarity with similar movements and persons of Christian orientation; (2) freedom for unions, "exempt from all political interference," with "class solidarity," rather than class struggle, their goal; (3) instilling in the workers an outlook that accords with Church teaching, which will make them cognizant of their role in the political community and prepared to "struggle against injustice and oppression, intolerance and absolutism by one man, one party, one sector, or one group of society or by the State"; and (4) the amelioration of the condition of workers, based on three essential values: *"Dios, Patria, Hogar"* (God, Country, Home).[16]

The President of the Federation, don Juan Ireneo Gonzáles, a traditionalist Catholic, actively oversees the projects of the 157 Argentinian *círculos,* which include low-income housing, various institutes, and numerous sports fields. When asked his opinion of the structural revolution advocated by the Movement of Priests for the Third World, his answer was emphatic: "There is only one world. To change it, revolutions or decrees are not enough. We must first change the individual. It is the task of religion and priests to aid in this transformation. On matters of a technical nature, we have our own experts." (For example, he cited a just-completed course on the theory and practice of unionism, conducted by Rubén Rotondaro of the American Institute for Free Labor Development, author of a recent book on the labor movement.) He repeatedly stressed his view that faith without action is dead, alluding to the MPTW's predilection for political agitation as opposed to con-

---

[15]*Labaro* (Buenos Aires), February 1962, No. 186, pp. 1-16.
[16]*Labaro,* March 1967, No. 234, pp. 20-21; *Federación de Círculos Católicos de Obreros. 80 Aniversario de su Fundación* (Buenos Aires, 1972), pp. 11-44.

crete accomplishments. In his opinion, political consciousness-raising among the masses is not a religious act, but an invitation to subversion and crime.[17] In this connection, he mentioned the assassination of former President Aramburu, in which Fr. Carbone of the MPTW had been implicated, and which had evoked a strong condemnation from him and the board of directors of the *círculos de obreros,* clearly aimed at the MPTW:

> The drama that has just stirred our country with the useless and condemnable sacrifice of life is another stage of the planned violence which, although it has its physical perpetrators, is also the result of the instigation of those who, with greater responsibility, maintain that violence is the only solution to obtain what they . . . call the just aspirations of the weaker economic strata of society. . . . They mold the declarations of the hierarchy and even of . . . Vatican II to justify their aims. . . .Therefore, the Federation of Círculos Católicos de Obreros repudiates all those . . . who make violence the means of the struggle for the elevation of the condition of life, which surely should be improved, but not by that means . . . .[18]

The Argentinian bishopric on occasion has supported the actions of the priests of the MPTW; the bishops have also taken the initiative themselves in various forms of social action. The late Bishop Miguel de Andrea, founder of the Argentine Professional Confederation (1913), the Popular Catholic Union of Argentina (1918), and the Federation of Catholic Associations of Female Employees (1922), was well known for his successful arbitration of several labor conflicts.[19] In 1955 he was arrested by Perón, and his house and church were burned. In more recent times, Bishops Alberto Devoto, Italo DiStefano, Enrique Angelelli, Carlos Cafferata, and Jaime de Nevares have been particularly active among the workers. Bishop Cafferata and thirty-two diocesan priests denounced the social injustices occurring in their diocese, and dismissed the governor's denials of the existence of such conditions. Bishop Nevares made several protests against the unsatisfactory working conditions of the construction workers on the El Chocon dam, and in 1971 refused to participate in its inauguration.[20]

Notwithstanding its sympathy with some of the MPTW's social concerns, the Argentine hierarchy rejects many of its fundamental assumptions and tactics, which clearly go beyond the workers' and Church's aims. Therefore, after individual bishops had warned the MPTW on several occasions to curtail their activities, a more official intervention was inevitable.

---

[17]Floridi interview with don Juan Ireneo Gonzáles, Buenos Aires, September 20, 1971.
[18]*Esquiú* (Buenos Aires), August 9, 1970.
[19]*Il Regno* (Bologna), February 1, 1968, pp. 70-71; Ofelia Siena Victorica de González del Solar, *Monseñor de Andrea* (Buenos Aires: FACE, n.d.), pp. 7-8.
[20]Alberto Delfico, "La Rebelión de los Marginados," in *Dinamis* (Buenos Aires weekly of the Sindicato Fuerza y Luz), April 1970, No. 19, pp. 16ff; and *Esquiú* (Buenos Aires), May 10, 1970.

On August 12, 1970, the Permanent Commission of the Argentine Hierarchy issued a declaration which, while not specifically naming the MPTW, singles out and condemns quotations from its manifestoes. "To join the revolutionary process," said the bishops, paraphrasing the MPTW, "calling for a Latin American brand of socialism that will necessarily mean socialization of the means of production, of economic and political power, and of culture, is improper and impermissible for any group of priests . . . ." Any priests who "maintain that authentic socialism will come to Latin America only when real revolutionaries, who come from the people and remain true to the people, seize power" are "inviting a social revolution, with all the violence inherent in it." Furthermore, such assertions entail "denying basic principles of the Church's social teaching." To substantiate their interpretation of Church teaching on the question of private ownership, the bishops quote from Pope John's encyclical *Mater et Magistra:*

> History and experience testify that where governments fail to recognize private ownership of goods, productive goods included, the fundamental manifestations of freedom are suppressed or stifled. . . . Hence one may justifiably conclude that the exercise of freedom finds both a guarantee and an incentive in the right of ownership.

However, the bishops add, this defense of the right of private ownership should not be taken to mean that they are "trying to preserve, much less to justify, the present state of things as if it were an expression of God's will." Nor are they trying to "protect the rich against the poor and needy," but are simply defending the "lofty ethico-social purpose of ownership."[21]

THE MPTW AND PERONISM

It is well known that for many years the Catholic Church supported Peronism, and only turned against it when it became apparent that Perón was determined to destroy those Catholic organizations not already under his sway. Few were the clergymen, such as de Andrea, who opposed Peronism from the outset. Thus, as Mecham noted, "it was not any conscious effort on the part of the Church which brought about a decision by Perón to alter his policy."[22] As Considine observed, "what a stain it would have been on the pages of history if Perón had come and gone and the Church was recorded as having bowed in subjection to the blandishments of the dictator."[23]

---

[21]*Esquiú* (Buenos Aires), April 23, 1970, in LADOC, December 1970, and *Polémica en la Iglesia. Documentos de Obispos Argentinos y Sacerdotes para el Tercer Mundo (1969-1970)* (Avellaneda, Argentina: Busqueda, 1970), pp. 27-39. See also the lengthy reply of the MPTW to the Permanent Commission of the Argentine hierarchy in the same book, pp. 41-123.

[22]J. Lloyd Mecham, *Church and State in Latin America,* rev. ed. (Chapel Hill, N.C.: University of North Carolina Press, 1966), p. 248.

[23]John J. Considine, *New Horizons in Latin America* (New York: Dodd, Mead and Co., 1958), viii.

Today, as indicated earlier in this chapter, priests—this time the members of the MPTW—are again leaning toward Peronism. Fr. Rolando Concatti, writing on the subject of "our choice of Peronism" on behalf of the MPTW, maintained that "Perón's myth finally redeems the revolutionary hope of the proletariat."[24] Initially, the priests of the MPTW debated whether Peronism could be considered "the" revolutionary vanguard, and the MPTW's allegiance to Peronism was not officially sanctioned, but was left up to the individual members. Some expressed their views openly, such as Fr. Milan Viscovic: "I stay with the Church of the CGT [Peronist labor movement], not with the Church of the chamber of commerce"—in other words, the Church of the poor against that of the rich; and Father Ruben Dri: "Peronism is the only truly popular force."[25]

For some, Perón's "third position" between capitalism and socialism was not sufficiently revolutionary; but with Perón's identification of his "third position" with *socialismo nacional,* the adherence of the MPTW to Peronism was ideologically consistent. Direct contacts with Perón eliminated any lingering doubts and uncertainties. Perón himself, flattered by the conversion of his old enemies, sent the MPTW a taped message in March 1969 which was reported by the Argentinian press, and in 1972 was published in an official MPTW compendium. In it he reviewed the struggle of his Justicialist movement "for social justice, economic independence and national sovereignty." He referred to the consistent opposition of the Argentine bishops, who "forgot the people, following the oligarchies instead." And he warmly praised the MPTW:

> You can imagine our satisfaction as we see the young priests of the MPTW joining us today in our unremitting struggle to defend the disinherited. Their presence in the slums and poverty belts created by the public authorities' neglect is a noble gesture that stirs our deepest solidarity; it is exactly what we have always sought.[26]

The subject of "socialism and Peronism" was thoroughly debated at the fourth meeting of the MPTW, which took place in Villa Carlos Paz (Córdoba) in July 1971, and at which 160 priests from thirty-six dioceses out of a total of forty-two participated. The MPTW priests denounced Argentina's leaders for betraying the nation to imperialism, for impoverishing the people, for the high rate of unemployment, and for the rapid disappearance of small industries. They charged that the Argentine revolution had deviated from the professed

---

[24]Rolando Concatti, *Neustra Opción por el Peronismo* (Mendoza, Argentina: SPTM, 1971), p. 34.
[25]Carlos A. Sacheri, *La Iglesia Clandestina* (Buenos Aires: Ed. del Cruzamante, 1970), pp. 99-101, and note 32.
[26]Rolando Concatti and Domingo Bresci, *Sacerdotes para el Tercer Mundo,* 3rd ed. (Buenos Aires: Publicaciones del MSTM, 1970), pp. 158-60.

goals of the armed forces, had not elevated the moral level of society, and therefore had failed. They attacked the labor leaders for "corruption of the union structures," and the Church hierarchy for attempting to slow down the process of popular liberation. Recognizing the "passivity" of the workers, the document approved the activities of the Revolutionary Peronist Movement, which it endowed with the capacity to achieve the objectives of the working class; at the same time it condemned those who used the term "Peronism" to "entrap the people in another of the lures set by the capitalist system."[27]

While Peronism is the most important political and trade union force in Argentina today, the role of labor within the new power structure is uncertain. Perón has always been able to divide and rule the labor leaders, who believe that his appeal to their rank and file exceeds their own. This accounts for the contradiction between organized labor's significant financial support of Peronism and its smaller representation at the political level.[28] Peronism's uneven record with regard to labor in the past—granting substantial gains in social security and wages, but restricting freedom of association and the rights to strike and bargain collectively and independently with employers—plus the Church's previous reversal on Peronism, suggest that the alignment of forces in support or opposition in the new chapter of Peronism in Argentina has not yet been determined.[29]

FR. CAMILO TORRES AND GUERRILLA VIOLENCE

Fr. Camilo Torres Restrepo of Colombia was the archetype guerrilla-priest in Latin America, with a legendary reputation akin to Che Guevara's. The son of an aristocratic mother and noted scientist father, he was a university student when, after spiritual meditation, he decided to become a priest. Immediately after his ordination he went to Louvain University in Belgium to specialize in the social sciences. During his stay in Europe he visited the famous Abbé Pierre in Paris, and became interested in his activities on behalf of the poor. In order to write his Ph.D. dissertation *(Statistical Investigation of the Socioeconomic Reality in the City of Bogotá)*, he returned briefly to Colombia in 1955. He became convinced of the necessity of convening a group

[27]*La Prensa* (Buenos Aires), July 11, 1971; see also Concatti and Bresci, *ibid.* pp. 167-74; and LADOC, September 1971.

[28]See *The New York Times,* March 17, 1973.

[29]See Juan José Taccone, "Los Sindicatos en la Argentina: Situación Actual y Perspectivas Futuras," in *CIAS* (Buenos Aires), December 1969, pp. 28-33; and T.S. Di Tella, "Stalemate or Coexistence in Argentina," in James Petras and Maurice Zeitlin, eds., *Latin America, Reform or Revolution?* (Greenwich, Connecticut: Fawcett Publications, 1968), pp. 259ff.

of experts to study the conditions of the country and to draw up proposals for concrete reforms. Therefore, following his return from Belgium in 1958, he founded the Movement of Students and Professionals for Community Organization (MUNIPROC). He was also instrumental in establishing the Faculty of Sociology of the National University. In June 1962 Fr. Torres published a defense of student protesters who had been expelled from the university. As a result of this action Cardinal Luis Concha Córdoba compelled him to leave his teaching post. Fr. Torres obeyed, stating that "it would be extremely painful for him to be considered a banner for secular struggles."[30]

What, then, finally propelled Fr. Torres into politics and then into guerrilla activities? Undoubtedly his frustration in the face of the immobilism prevalent in his country. One day he told some friends: "Here nobody moves to make the revolution; I feel like throwing away my cassock and starting this revolution myself."[31] This exclamation is a revealing clue to Fr. Torres' personality, and to how he did ultimately become, almost unwittingly, "a banner for secular struggles." Early in 1965 he began to prepare a platform around which to unite all those persuaded of the need for structural reform (Catholics, Communists and members of other political parties, workers, peasants, and students). The platform is essentially radical and utopian in nature. Concerning the workers, it stated:

> Free enterprise will be abolished and replaced by cooperative and communitarian enterprise. . . . All the workers will be able to be shareholders. . . . Pluralism in union organization will be encouraged, always allowing for the free choice of the workers. Freedom for the organization of labor will be respected in keeping with international labor organization agreements. . . .[32]

Torres envisaged the establishment of a United Front of Popular Movements. At the local level action committees were to be formed; the leaders of these local committees were to then meet and elect delegates for a national conference in Bogotá to plan the immediate objectives and electoral strategy of the United Front. As events transpired, Torres erred in believing that he would be able to rally around his platform in a few months' time the divergent factions to which he appealed. At the same time the inevitable clash with the hierarchy forced him to ask permission to leave the priesthood. This contributed to alienating many of the practicing Catholics. Accused of having become a Communist, he declared:

> I have said that as a Colombian citizen, as a sociologist, as a Christian and as a priest, I am a revolutionary. I think that the Communist

---

[30]Norberto Habegger, *Camilo Torres, Prete e Guerrigliero* (Florence, Italy: Cultura Editrice, 1968), p. 37.

[31]*Ibid.*, p. 38.

[32]J. Álvarez García and C. Restrepo Calle, eds., *Camilo Torres, His Life and His Message* (Springfield, Illinois: Templegate Publishers, 1968), pp. 60-67.

Party has truly revolutionary elements and, therefore, as a Colombian citizen, as a sociologist, and as a priest I cannot be anticommunist.[33]

It is evident that in Camilo Torres' program revolutionary politics took precedence over religion. Torres himself and his magazine *Frente Unido* transmitted his message of the urgency of revolution throughout the country and to the various sectors of Colombian society. In his message to the labor unions he spoke of the unity of the "laboring masses . . . along with many of the leaders, around the platform of the United Front." He urged the workers to use their financial resources and organizing abilities to mobilize the entire proletariat, and severely criticized those union leaders who prevented the workers from joining the United Front. This was a direct attack not only against the leaders of the UTC, but especially against the priests who were its "spiritual advisers" and against the bishops who supported it over the ASA and CLASC (which supported Torres).

Echoes of this controversy were evident in an article by the founder of the UTC, Fr. Vicente Andrade; in the vigorous rebuttal by an official of the International Federation of Christian Trade Unions (now the World Confederation of Labor), and in the equally strong surrebuttal by Fr. Andrade. The IFCTU official protested Andrade's implication that European Catholics, through CLASC, plus the Communist Party, had financed Camilo Torres' campaign. Andrade retorted:

> The most unfortunate aspect of what has been going on in Colombia . . . is that, because of CLASC's blundering activities and the refusal of the international directors of the IFCTU to see this problem, the Catholic social movement has been stymied and Communism has gained . . . when choosing between the unanimous judgment of the Colombian bishops and Catholic leaders on the one hand, and the unyielding and mistaken position of the small group of CLASC members on the other, these directors of the IFCTU have consistently sided with the latter. . . .[34]

In the midst of this controversy, the Christian Social Democratic Party, CLASC, the ASA, and certain other parties and unions began to have serious doubts about the possibility of realizing the type of coalition advocated by the United Front. The first signs of the split appeared at a conference held in Medellín in September 1965, during which Fr. Torres tried to unite the opposing groups. The debate was particularly heated over what strategy to adopt in the forthcoming elections: abstention, revolutionary struggle through legal pressures and the exercise of workers' social power, or armed uprisings. Abstention prevailed, and this fact worried Fr. Torres.

---

[33]Norberto Habegger, *op. cit.*, pp. 55ff; see also pp. 70-72 and p. 84.
[34]Fr. Andrade's original article appeared in *America* (New York), September 18, 1965, p. 287. The rebuttal, by A. Vanistendael, and Andrade's surrebuttal appeared in the same publication, November 6, 1965, pp. 512-13.

Not long afterward, several groups, chiefly those of Christian orientation, began to withdraw from the United Front. The week following the Medellín meeting, the Christian Social Democratic Party and CLASC both withdrew. The ASA returned to the anticommunist position of proposing a. Christian united front to "realize the inevitable revolution." In reality, writes one of Torres' biographers, the Christian Social Democratic Party was actually looking for a way to participate in the election.[35] This version of the events surrounding Torres' efforts to create a united front conflicts with assertions of Emilio Máspero, Secretary General of CLAT, who has stated that his organization remained "with Fr. Torres to the end."[36]

Torres' messages of November and December reveal that he had abandoned hope of uniting the opposition forces and was considering joining the guerrillas in the mountains. It was about this time that he joined the Army of National Liberation, founded by secessionists from the Moscow-oriented Communist Party. On February 15, 1966, Camilo Torres died in an ambush by a patrol of the regular army.

Asked his opinion of Camilo Torres, Brazilian Archbishop Dom Helder Câmara replied:

> He was a sincere priest, but then he found his dream shattered that the Church really wanted to put into practice its beautiful texts about justice. He thought that the Communist Party was the only one that could do anything. But the Communists sent him into combat so that he would be killed: they figured that with his death Colombia would burst into flames. But that didn't happen. When they finally killed him, nobody stirred.[37]

PRIEST AND NUN GUERRILLAS
IN COLOMBIA, BOLIVIA, GUATEMALA, URUGUAY, AND BRAZIL

Colombia. The philosophy of Camilo Torres was embraced in Colombia by a group of about fifty priests, who called themselves the Golconda Movement after the farm where they first met in July 1968. Between then and July 1970 they met four times, before officially deciding to disband because of factionalism within their ranks. However, vestiges of the movement remain active underground.

At its second meeting (Buenaventura, December 9-13, 1968) the group issued a treatise known as the Golconda Declaration, signed by forty-eight

---

[35]Norberto Habegger, *op. cit.,* p. 83.

[36]Giovanni Gozzer, *Religione e Rivoluzione in America Latina* (Milan: Bompiani, 1968), pp. 182-84. In the Dominican Republic a splinter group that has broken away from the CLAT affiliate, CASC, seeking to cover itself with the Torres mantle, has taken the name "Camilistas."

[37]Interview with Oriana Fallaci, *Siete Días Ilustrados* (Buenos Aires), October 5, 1970, in LADOC, June 1971.

priests and the then Bishop of Buenaventura, Gerardo Valencia Cano. The document called for the overthrow "by a genuine revolution" of Colombia's capitalist oligarchy; the abolition of political and economic dependency on the United States; and the replacement of existing structures by a socialist society. It urged the implementation of agrarian reform, to give the masses "access to the land and a share in the nation's production"; and urban reform, "which must be one of the first targets in a radical change of structures." In order to achieve its ends, the Golconda Movement pledged: "We irrevocably commit ourselves to every manner of revolutionary action against imperialism and the neo-colonial bourgeoisie."[38]

Like other leftist Catholic groups already discussed, the Golconda Movement believed it necessary to transcend the social doctrine of the Church. As one of its members, Fr. Noel Olaya, wrote:

> The so-called social doctrine of the Catholic Church rejects class struggle, preaching instead union and reconciliation among all classes. But that is pure reformism: it does not question the social structures as such, it limits itself to suggesting certain surface reforms that will make them less scandalous.[39]

Under the influence of Marxist theoretician Germán Zabala, the Golconda faction that published *Frente Unido*, led by Fathers René García, Luis Currea, Manuel Alzate and Vicente Mejía, warned: The dialogue that takes place in this movement between Christians and Marxists is not an intellectual luxury. The unifying theme for all is "to ascend to the masses" and to learn from them the tactics, strategy, and timing of the revolution. Certain groups within the traditional left which pursue their goals within the existing social structure desire to subsume any mass-based movement such as Golconda within their own movement. However, "in the opinion of Golconda, revolutionaries who fail to learn from the masses run the grave risk of sectarian elitism or 'groupism.' "[40]

The Golconda group's call to action caused one of its members, a Spanish priest by the name of Fr. Domingo Laín, to join the Army of National Liberation, the guerrilla movement to which Camilo Torres also belonged. Charged with using secret subversive codes, Laín was expelled from his Cartagena parish in March 1969, and deported to Spain. Shortly thereafter, however, he re-entered Colombia illegally and became a guerrilla. Upon joining the guerrillas, he declared:

---

[38]*Catholic Mind*, March 1970, in LADOC, June 1970. See also *Iglesia Latinoamericana: ¿Protesta o Profecía?*, pp. 226-35; *America*, March 4, 1972, pp. 235-37; *Time Magazine*, April 23, 1973. Bishop Gerardo Valencia Cano died in an airplane accident on January 21, 1972.

[39]CIDOC 71/327, in LADOC, January 1972.

[40]René García Lizarralde,"Habla Golconda:¿Toda la Iglesia en la Revolución?" in *Núcleo* (Bogotá), No. 37, September 12, 1969, and *NACLA Newsletter,* (Berkeley, California), February 1970; see also "Fr. R. Garcia Speaks to Colombian Students," in LADOC, November 1970.

In making my decision public, I am only renewing the irrevocable commitment that I accepted when I was ordained a priest: dedication and fidelity to the poor and the oppressed, solidarity in their struggle for liberation from all slavery.[41]

Another Colombian priest, Fr. Pedro Ramón Prada, announced his decision to join the guerrilla movement in the summer of 1971 during a meeting of extremists celebrating the anniversary of the Communist Party.[42] The arrest of a Swedish reporter as a Soviet spy in the summer of 1972 led to the discovery of an urban guerrilla network which also included several priests.[43]

The situation in Colombia is complicated by the authorities' linkage of other elements in the Church with the guerrillas. One such incident prompted an angry statement by the superiors of the Jesuit Order following the arrest (and subsequent release) of one of their members for his role in assisting a group of Manatí peasants press their claim to some land. In their statement the Jesuits declared:

> The Manatí incidents offer us the opportunity to ponder a . . . more urgent problem, a symptom of which is the social injustice which . . . is rooted in the nation's socioeconomic and legal structures. . . . it deeply concerns us that in Colombia forces exist that attempt to muzzle evangelist liberty; their methods range from the most subtle form of labeling as subversives or rebels all priests involved in the social apostolate, to jailing them. . . . Our participation in the creation of a new social order presupposes in us a continuous conversion to God and to our brethren, to take place in a climate of mounting involvement with the poor and the oppressed.[44]

The Colombian government has announced several times the annihilation of the rebels, but there are sporadic resurgences of guerrilla activity. The army still has occasional skirmishes with three guerrilla bands: the Army of National Liberation (ELN), the Revolutionary Armed Forces of Colombia (FARC) and the Popular Liberation Army (EPL).

Bolivia. The news that three Colombian nuns of the Laurita Order, headquartered at Medellín, Colombia, had been arrested and expelled from Bolivia in May 1972, caused a sensation. The government charged that guerrillas were living and working in the convent school and other social centers. A sizable cache of arms and munitions, some belonging to the Bolivian Army, was discovered in the convent. Cardinal Clemente Maurer of La Paz, who

---

[41]Quoted by Fr. Javier Darío Restrepo, *Revista Familia* (Bogota), April 1970, and LADOC, November 1970. The magazine was thereupon banned in the archdiocese of Medellín and the author was suspended by the bishop.

[42]*El País* (Cali, Colombia), July 16, 1971.

[43]*El Siglo* (Bogotá), July 19, 1972.

[44]Press release of the Jesuit Order in Colombia, August 10, 1972.

has defended members of the clergy accused of subversion,[45] criticized the actions of the deported nuns: "As the Church has stated, we cannot agree with the activities of delinquents, as in the recent case of the ousted Laurita Sisters, and we certainly cannot approve of such behavior."[46] Mother Margaret Ochoa, Superior General of the Lauritas, not only abhored the involvement of the three nuns, but said that they had been misled by a "theology of liberation" and had "deviated" from the aims of the community. Nevertheless, the Latin American Pastoral Institute (IPLA), an organ of CELAM located in Ecuador, issued a statement signed by fifty-five scholars from twelve Latin American countries criticizing Mother Margaret. Her action, they declared, was "an affront to evangelism"; the nuns were demonstrating "a faithful understanding of the search for adaptation of structures and mode of life aimed at more effectively serving the poor and oppressed without losing touch with the order's founding spirit."[47]

"Nuns of Latin America face an identity crisis" was the conclusion of a survey published shortly after the Lauritas' expulsion from Bolivia by the Latin American Confederation of Religion (CLAR), an organ of CELAM. The CLAR study underlined the sociological implications of the fact that approximately a quarter of the 131,000 sisters working in an area torn by social, economic, political and cultural discontent are not indigenous to the area, and deplored the fact that most of the work performed by nuns in Latin America is foreign-directed.[48]

Guatemala. The problems that may ensue from the presence of large numbers of foreign clergymen in Latin America are illustrated also by the expulsion from Guatemala of two American priests and a nun of the Maryknoll Order, for alleged complicity in guerrilla activities.[49] The expelled missionaries

---

[45]Since the overthrow of the government of General Juan José Torres in August 1971, Church-State relations in Bolivia have become increasingly tense. Cardinal Maurer and several bishops have protested the arrest of priests who were charged with "preaching communism." See *The Pilot* (Boston) March 25, April 15 and 29, and May 13, 1972. After the Cardinal met with Colonel Hugo Banzer, the Bolivian President, the situation seemed improved. The arrests at the Laurita convent were made with his knowledge. But the subsequent arrest of a German priest, Fr. Klaus Weber, who had been in charge of several colonization and development programs since 1967, marked another setback in Church-State relations (*The Pilot*, August 5, 1972). On Bolivian guerrillas see R. Vásquez Díaz, *La Bolivia del Che* (Milan: Jaca Book, 1968). Recently the press has reported the imprisonment, torture, and deportation of a former Maryknoll nun, Mary Harding, who had been involved in union work in La Paz, and had left the order to aid the Army for National Liberation (*New York Times*, January 11, 1973, and *Miami Herald*, May 16, 1973).

[46]*The Pilot* (Boston), June 3 and 24, 1972. On June 28, 1972, the Bolivian press announced that Cochabamba Bishop Armando Gutiérrez had protested to the Bolivian President about raids in search of guerrillas at a church and convent.

[47]*National Catholic Register* (Los Angeles, California), July 30, 1972.

[48]*The Pilot,* July 29, 1972.

[49]Francis X. Gannon, "Catholicism, Revolution and Violence in Latin America: Lessons of 1968 Guatemala Maryknoll Episode," *Orbis,* pp. 1204-1225.

admitted to their superiors in Guatemala that twice in late 1967 they met with guerrilla leaders and discussed the possibility of linking their efforts.[50] In defending their actions, they justified revolutionary violence by the Guatemalan masses because it is "the oligarchy that is using violence—that is, violating the rights of the masses."[51]

The Jesuits of the Centro de Adiestramiento para Promotores Sociales (a social work training center which uses the technique of *conscientização*) at Landivar University, while strongly criticizing the government and the Church, reject the notion that guerrilla violence is the only solution for Guatemala. Professor René de León Schlotter of the Universidad de San Carlos, specialist in labor law and problems of development, has also refuted the guerrilla thesis that there can be no thought of development until after the people are liberated from exploitation. What the guerrillas fail to understand, he has asserted, is that violence, even when in the name of justice, is always counterproductive as a means of liberation.[52]

When the Guatemalan authorities decided to deport the priests and nun, the Maryknoll Superiors announced to the press that they had "personally interfered in the internal affairs of a country where we are guests, thus violating a strict policy of the order." In a signed statement all 102 Maryknollers in Guatemala disassociated themselves from the actions of the expelled members:

> We wish to make known our opposition to the naive, impetuous and romantic reasoning which has now set back the authentic work of human and social development in Guatemala. . . . Here, guerrillas and revolution mean kidnapping, murder, machine-gunning, stealing, bombing of school buses.[53]

Uruguay. In this country the separation of Church and State came peacefully in 1919. There is no concordat with the Vatican and clergymen do not enjoy any special status. Because of this secular atmosphere, "the Catholic Church of Uruguay has lent itself mostly to things spiritual and social," leaving politics to the layman.[54] Nonetheless, the example of Camilo Torres has found numerous sympathizers among the Uruguayan clergy. According to a publication on the Tupamaro guerrillas, a priest was killed while trying to purchase

---

[50]Gannon, *op. cit.* p. 1215, reporting newspaper accounts and an "unidentified Maryknoll spokesman."

[51]*Ibid.,* p. 1217.

[52]Floridi interview with René de León Schlotter, May 17, 1971. His views are also expressed in a recent book published by the Instituto para el Desarrollo Económico-social de América Central (IDESAC), Nelson Amaro, ed., *El Reto del Desarrollo en Guatamela* (Guatemala City: Publicaciones IDESAC, 1970), p. 9.

[53]In Thomas and Marjorie Melville, *Whose Heaven, Whose Earth?* (New York: Alfred A. Knopt, 1971), pp. 283-84.

[54]M. Alisky, *Uruguay, A Contemporary Survey* (New York: Frederick A. Praeger, 1969), p. 85.

typewriters and a mimeograph machine for the guerrillas.[55] Another Uruguayan priest and a former Jesuit, Fr. Juan Carlos Zaffaroni, like Camilo Torres advocated armed struggle. He traveled to Havana to participate, with Mgr. Guzman (Colombia), Fr. Escuardia (Mexico) and Fr. Blanquart (France) in the Congress of the Intellectuals, a meeting of Latin Americans and Europeans in January 1968 to define the role of intellectuals in the revolution. During the conference, Fidel Castro read to the participants a statement by these four priests, in which they declared:

> Father Camilo Torres Restrepo, with his death for the revolution, has given the highest example of loyalty to the popular cause; now, therefore, we support the revolutionary anti-imperialist struggle to its ultimate consequences, in order to uphold the cause of liberation of the whole world and of all men . . . .[56]

Fr. Zaffaroni was subsequently reprimanded by his religious superiors for having publicly incited people to revolt, and went underground in order to avoid arrest.[57]

When the Tupamaros kidnapped a Brazilian diplomat and murdered U.S. official Dan Mitrione in 1970, Fr. Justo Asiaín Márquez was arrested for having been in contact with the guerrillas. Later a Uruguayan priest, Fr. Uberfils Monzón, a CELAM representative, was arrested and tortured by the Paraguayan police who suspected him of being a Tupamaro.[58]

In 1972, following the election of President Juan María Bordaberry and the declaration of a "state of internal war," Church-State relations became more strained. On April 18, 1972 the Coadjutor Archbishop of Montevideo, Carlos Parteli, and other Catholic clergymen attended the funeral of seven Communists killed the preceding day in a confrontation with the armed forces. Two days later, Fr. Arnaldo Spadaccino and Fr. Luis Rodríguez were arrested after a raid on the Latin American Catholic Students' Secretariat, where the Catholic leftist magazine *Víspera* is printed. With the capture of more Tupamaro units and the discovery of additional guerrilla hideouts and documents, more priests were arrested. A Spanish priest, Fr. Carlos Fernández Ordóñez, who handled propaganda for the Tupamaros, was jailed

---

[55]*The Tupamaros, Urban Guerrilla Warfare in Uruguay* (New York: The Liberated Guardian, n.d.), pp. 48-49.

[56]See *Il Regno* (Bologna), March 1, 1968, p. 116, and Carl Oglesby, *The New Left Reader* (New York: Grove Press, 1969), p. 119.

[57]Alain Gheerbrant, *L'Eglise Rebelle d'Amerique Latine* (Paris: Editions du Seuil, 1969), pp. 276-89.

[58]Alain Labrousse, *Les Tupamaros. Guerrilla Urbaine en Uruguay* (Paris: Editions du Seine, 1971), p. 163. Excerpts from a recent book, *Tupamaros Guerrillas*, by Uruguayan newspaperwoman Maria Esther Guiliu, were published by the French weekly *L'Express* (Paris), January 31, 1972. Fr. Monzón describes these events in *Perspectivas de Diálogo* (Montevideo), April-May 1971, in LADOC, November 1971.

with forty other guerrillas.[59] Among the members of the Tupamaro "Column 22," uncovered in the departments of Rivera and Tacuarembo, was Fr. Roberto Guillermo Verissimo, parish priest of the Santo Domingo Chapel in Rivera Chico, who carried out surveillance of police headquarters and personnel.[60] On another list of Tupamaros prosecuted by the military court were the names of an ex-priest, Nestor Alesio Saravi Díaz, and Fr. Pier Luigi Murgoni, an Italian professor of mathematics, who performed technical work in electronics for the organization.[61]

The Permanent Committee of the Uruguayan Episcopal Conference (CEU), presided over by Archbishop Parteli, blamed both the guerrillas and the government for these events: "The radical demands made by the subversive groups is another symptom to be added to those that already indicated serious defects in our social organization." They warned the state to "rapidly initiate" the necessary changes, and condemned the torture of prisoners by the security forces. And they aligned the Church with those who advocate "great changes" in the country, based on the "Christian sentiment" of the people.[62]

Brazil. As already noted, the revolutionary theories and actions of some Latin American priests have at times outstripped those of the secular revolutionaries. This clerical radicalism is exemplified by some of the ideas of Fr. Joseph Comblin, a Belgian priest who, until March 1972 (when he was barred from returning to Brazil), was a professor of theology at the Seminary of Recife.

Fr. Comblin expressed his theories in a memorandum to Archbishop Dom Helder Câmara, prior to the latter's departure for the Medellín Conference.[63] When this document was published many were shocked by its recommendations: Church support for guerrilla warfare; resort to authoritarian and dictatorial power in the initial stages of the revolution; exile of wealthy persons who refused to make sacrifices; and Church willingness to "dip [its] hands in dirty alliances."

Fr. Comblin dismissed the possibility of achieving fundamental reforms through normal political evolution. Rather, the State, exercising totalitarian power, would have to impose the new structures by destroying the existing privileges of the few. Moreover, once the new structures were in place the exercise of political power would require a "repressive system" of special

---

[59]*Diario de Minas* (Brazil), June 3, 1972.

[60]*La Mañana* (Montevideo), June 19, 1972.

[61]*El País* (Montevideo), June 23, 1972.

[62]*El País*, June 16, 1972; President Bordaberry's reply appears in the same issue.

[63]*Estado de Minas* (Brazil), July 9, 1968. Charles Antoine says the "Comblin Document" was the result of a special pre-conference study requested by Dom Helder; *in Church and Power in Brazil* (Maryknoll, N.Y.: Orbis Books, 1973), p. 146.

courts to try the opposition, since "radical reforms cannot be passed by consulting the majority."

Not all of Fr. Comblin's recommendations, however, were of the same tenor. On the subject of the workers and unions, he wrote:

> Socialization will require a different effort for the lower classes: they will have to accept the discipline of technical work, to renounce patriarchal ways, individualism, and the ideals of becoming small businessmen. They will have to accept hard work, and the will of the majority in union activities. Everyone will have to cooperate in a disciplined manner with a strong government, and . . . renounce negative criticism.

He called on the Church to devote its educational activities, instead of to the preservation of the status quo, to instilling the values of a developed society: by teaching technical and productive skills, by upgrading agricultural practices, and by promoting vocational training, education, and research. Finally, Fr. Comblin prodded the Church to make itself more relevant to the changing needs of the people if it wants to survive, and if it hopes to prevent the masses from marching to the tune of a different drummer:

> There is no doubt that the traditional Catholic religious feelings of the people are going to disappear with development. If the Church will not have a more advanced religion to offer, the masses will look elsewhere to other messages more concerned and closer to them.[64]

Another revelation that stunned Brazilian public opinion was the news that Carlos Marighela, a leftist politician and follower of Fidel Castro, had been killed on his way to a meeting with some Dominican monks.[65] Two days before Marighela's death the police had found in the possession of two monks arrested in Rio de Janeiro a notebook indicating that they received Marighela's messages in their bookstore in São Paulo. The police then intercepted a message setting up a meeting between the monks and Marighela. They ordered the monks to keep the appointment, and ambushed Marighela as he arrived. The monks said that they had not participated directly in the robberies and murders committed by Marighela's Ação Libertadora Nacional (ALN). Cardinal Scherer, Archbishop of Porto Alegre, disagreed, contending that it was inconceivable that they had not known who Marighela was and what he was doing: the press had reported his expulsion from the pro-Soviet Brazilian Communist Party (PCB) as a Castro sympathizer and believer in armed struggle. In fact, it is likely that the monks themselves arranged the publication abroad of Marighela's book on guerrilla strategy and tactics. Ironically, in his book

---

[64]*Estado de Minas* (Brazil), July 9, 1968. See also Fr. Comblin's article in *Revue Nouvelle* (Belgium), May-June 1972, and his book *Jesus de Nazare* (Petropolis, Brazil: Vozes, 1971), in which he explains his updating of Christianity; and Bishop João E. Enout's critique in *Liturgia e Vida* (Brazil), January-February 1972, pp. 18-26.

[65]*O Estado de São Paulo,* November 5, 1969.

Marighela warns of the risk of police infiltration when one is collaborating with persons of unknown backgrounds, and the importance for a revolutionary to avoid commiting anything to paper—both of which were his undoing in the fatal ambush.[66]

How representative are these radical priests? How much following do they have? In all countries the priests and movements discussed in this chapter represent a small proportion of the total clergy, but, while there is no uniform trend, indications are that their number is growing.

At the same time, opposition to these movements continues to be expressed by both clergy and laymen. In Mexico the local branch of Chile's Movement of Christians for Socialism and the Mexican Priests for People were assailed by Bishop Arturo Vélez Martínez at a pilgrimage of 60,000 laymen for having "gone to negative extremes." The St. Pius X Priests' Association at a national convention in Teptitlán, Mexico, declared that it was "vigorously denouncing those false trends of error which are capturing many naive priests, who seek an easy way to shun their priestly duties."[67]

However, in countries where many are casting about for new and viable alternatives to what they consider the discredited past attempts to solve the problems of dependence and economic underdevelopment, the impact of these movements exceeds their actual size. The recent creation of a Latin American Federation of Priests' Movements—grouping the Argentinian Movement of Priests of the Third World, the Chilean Movement of Christians for Socialism, the Peruvian ONIS Movement, and the Mexican Priests for People—will undoubtedly further extend their influence.[68] The establishment of this federation may also be an attempt by these movements to forestall the expansion of the more extremist groups, and to preclude possible condemnation by the bishops.

---

[66]*Dossier sul Brasile. A Cura del Centro Azione e Documentazione sull' America Latina* (Milan: Ediz. Sapere, 1970), pp. 165-66.
[67]*National Catholic Register,* March 25, 1973.
[68]*Ibid.,* April 1, 1973.

IV
CONCLUSION: WORKER ATTITUDES
AND CHURCH OPTIONS

The unspoken questions underlying this review of the relationship between the Catholic Church and the Catholic-oriented labor unions in Latin America are, first, what do the workers themselves think of these movements and ideologies which are espoused by the various segments of the clergy and labor organizations, and, second, how should the Church respond to these worker attitudes? While the response of the workers is of fundamental importance, it is also difficult to gauge. A few studies of worker attitudes have been conducted using scientific survey techniques, but in general this is an area meriting much additional research.

In fact, what we are seeking to determine is, how revolutionary is Latin American labor? The importance of this question was emphasized by Wendell C. Gordon: "Whether in the future the labor unions of Latin America are going to be essentially pragmatic or essentially political and revolutionary is one of the really important questions in the Latin American field."[1] Implicit throughout this study has been the hypothesis that Latin American workers, specifically those affiliated with various types of unions of Catholic orientation, support a reformist approach to social change, and reject the ideology and tactics of violent revolution advocated by the most radical elements within the Latin American clergy. What kind of evidence can be marshalled to support or refute this interpretation?

ATTITUDES OF LATIN AMERICAN WORKERS

In their seminal study published in 1960, *Industrialism and Industrial Man,* Clark Kerr and his colleagues postulated that workers tend to become more moderate and less ideological in the course of industrialization; a decade later the authors reiterated this hypothesis, and even strengthened their conclusion concerning the increasing conservatism of workers: "We would now add that they tend to become more moderate than we once envisaged, some indeed becoming conservative members of the body politic."[2]

---

[1]"The Latin American Labor Movement," in Stanley M. Davis and Louis W. Goodman, eds., *Workers and Managers in Latin America* (Lexington, Massachusetts: D.C. Heath and Co., 1972), p. 240.

[2]"Industrialism and Industrial Man: A Postscript," *International Labour Review,* Vol. 103, No. 6, June 1961. One unexplored area meriting investigation is whether the existence of CLAT and its probable future policies will disprove the hypothesis of the increasing conservatism of workers as economic development accelerates. CLAT believes that "the true nature of the problems confronting the Latin American working man does not stem from low wages, but rather from the unjust social and economic system in which he operates," and that concentrating on immediate issues diverts organized labor from its more legitimate and important economic, social, and political objectives. This philosophy may deter substantial new affiliations, which casts some doubt on the likely success of CLAT's goal of serving as a catalyst to organize and mobilize the workers into a lower-class pressure group. Michael J. Francis, "Revolutionary Labor in Latin America: The CLASC," *Journal of Inter-American Studies,* p. 598.

The question of whether or not labor is revolutionary can, of course, degenerate into semantic disagreement, which detracts from the comparability of the studies. Such is the case of the apparent differences in interpretation of Landsberger and Alexander. Alexander maintains that Latin American labor is indeed revolutionary:

> Organized labor in Latin America has had an essentially revolutionary role. It has been a part of the movement for basic economic, social, and political change, and has represented a group which was seeking a larger role in the general life of the community.[3]

Landsberger, restricting his definition of the term "revolutionary" to those "groups which explicitly have as their goal substantial changes in major social institutions, such as the property system or the system of access to political power," qualifies Alexander's assessment. He suggests that "labor is revolutionary only in some, albeit important, meanings of that term but definitely not in others . . . . We maintain that labor's basic aims are mundane ones: shortrange, limited, economic, and not primarily the total reconstruction of society." Therefore, Landsberger concludes, labor is neither as "ideologized" nor as "revolutionary" as in the past. His evidence for this assertion is the decline in the number of separate labor federations founded on the basis of distinct, generally revolutionary, doctrines. The possibility of merger across former ideological barriers indicates *de facto* a decline in the salience of ideology. Thus, in Landberger's view,

> the desire to pressure for improved conditions, and any success in doing so, is in itself revolutionary. But in the more extreme, more usual sense of this term—that of supporting ideologies which demand changes in power and property relations, explicitly as a necessary first step and not merely as an implicit concomitant of the recognition of labor's demands—Latin American labor has usually not been revolutionary.[4]

Another difficulty in comparing the findings of the studies of worker attitudes is the frequent absence of like units of comparison. For example, the present study, like that of Lodge,[5] includes organizations of agrarian workers, and even the loosely-structured peasant bands, while Alexander and Landsberger, as well as the authors of some of the country studies,[6] limit themselves to organized workers, i.e., generally urban and/or industrial work-

---

[3]Robert J. Alexander, *Organized Labor in Latin America* (New York: The Free Press, 1965, p. 12.

[4]Henry A. Landsberger, "The Labor Elite: Is it Revolutionary?" in Seymour Martin Lipset and Aldo Solari, eds., *Elites in Latin America* (New York: Oxford University Press, 1967), pp. 263-69.

[5]George C. Lodge, *Engines of Change* (New York: Alfred A. Knopf, 1970).

[6]For example, James L. Payne, *Labor and Politics in Peru. The System of Political Bargaining* (New Haven: Yale University Press, 1965).

ers. Since Lodge, for example, specifically contrasts the more revolutionary nature of the agrarian worker organizations with these older, more conventional, more established unions, it is important to ascertain what type or types of unions one is discussing.

Having registered these caveats, we can now proceed to summarize the findings of several of the more informative studies of worker attitudes.

Landsberger, seeking evidence of attitudes of Latin American labor *leaders*, could cite "only two attitude surveys of Latin American labor elites sufficiently systematic to be taken as reliable sources of information."[7] The first is the study of conflict and concensus attitudes among Venezuelan elites, including 235 labor leaders, conducted by the Centro de Estudios del Desarrollo (Center for Development Studies—CENDES) of the Universidad Central de Venezuela, in collaboration with Frank Bonilla of the Center for International Studies of M.I.T.[8] The second study is Landsberger's own survey of 231 presidents of blue-collar unions in Chile's three major industrial centers.[9] The universe of a third study, conducted by Alex Inkeles in Chile, includes rank and file members and non-unionized workers, in addition to thirty-seven union leaders.[10]

In Landsberger's study labor leaders' conceptions of the function of the union were probed in such a way as to permit the expression of: (1) a Marxist conception ("arouse the workers' political consciousness"); or (2) a traditional Catholic view ("improve the education and moral level of the workers"); as well as (3) responses concerned with the traditional bread-and-butter issues of higher salaries, improved working conditions, etc. Landsberger compares his findings with those of Inkeles as follows: 62 per cent of union leaders chose economic objectives as most important (54 per cent for Inkeles); the option of "arousing political awareness" was chosen first by only 0.8 per cent (3 per cent for Inkeles). The surprising feature of this breakdown is that, despite the fact that 43 per cent of the union leaders Landsberger inter-

---

[7]Landsberger, "The Labor Elite," p. 271. Some additional studies have been published since Landsberger's in 1964, but few have systematically attempted to correlate worker attitudes with political choice. One exception is "The Working-Class Vote in Chile: Christian Democracy versus Marxism," by Maurice Zeitlin and James Petras, which analyzes electoral returns in 296 Chilean municipalities in the 1958 and 1964 presidential elections. Using electoral statistics and ecological data, the authors adduce evidence to support their hypothesis that "the typical worker of Chile voted for FRAP [the Allende coalition] in 1958 and 1964. . . ."; in Davis and Goodman, *op. cit.*, pp. 249-57, and the *British Journal of Sociology*, March 1970, pp. 16-29.

[8]In Lipset and Solari, *op. cit.*, p. 271; see also J.A. Silva-Michelena, F. Bonilla, and J. Cotler, "La Investigación Sociológica y la Formulación de Políticas," *América Latina*, VIII, 2 (1965) pp. 2-47.

[9]These findings are reported in Davis and Goodman, *op. cit.*; Lipset and Solari, *op. cit.*; and in *Industrial and Labor Relations Review*, April 1964, Vol. 17, No. 3.

[10]Reported by Landsberger in Lipset and Solari, *op. cit.*, p. 272.

viewed professed to favor the two Chilean Marxist parties, the Communist and Socialist, they did not approach union matters from a Marxist perspective. On the other hand, while 23 per cent of the union leaders supported the Christian Democrats, only 8 per cent in Landsberger's study said that to "improve the educational and spiritual development of the workers" was the most important union goal.[11] In sum, labor leaders regard the union "chiefly as a tool to obtain economic benefits through collective bargaining; their Marxist or Catholic ideologies are not strong enough to guide them in their perception of the function of the union."[12]

In his study of Brazilian factory workers, Leôncio M. Rodrigues also asked several questions relating to workers' views of the proper role of, and their reasons for joining, a union.[13] The replies reveal a basically trade-unionist, non-class outlook among his respondents. Since the Brazilian labor code prescribes that unions may spend revenues derived from the trade union tax only for social welfare and legal assistance, it is not surprising that Rodrigues' respondents regarded these as the unions' principal legitimate functions. A total of 64 per cent said they joined the union primarily because of the availability of medical, dental, and legal services. Only 19 per cent listed defense of workers' interests, while another 10 per cent mentioned obtaining higher salaries as the most important reason. Thus, only 29 per cent of the respondents gave what could be considered "class" responses.[14] Again, when asked what advantages unions offer workers, social assistance (medical, dental, and legal) and salary augmentation far outranked defense of the workers' interests among both union members and nonmembers, and among skilled and semiskilled workers alike.[15]

The CENDES study also found that the same individuals who criticize the State, the parties, and the bureaucracy still expect that improvement of their condition will come from within the system. Forty-eight per cent of the respondents—by far the largest group—regarded violence against the government as "justified only if the government itself stepped outside the law." On the other hand, only one-third as many considered violence justified in the event the government "did not represent the interests of the people."[16]

A critical variable in determining whether organized labor maintains reformist, within-system goals, Landsberger emphasized, is the presence or absence of viable reformist options:

---

[11]In Davis and Goodman, *op. cit.*, p. 246.
[12]Landsberger, "The Labor Elite," p. 274.
[13]Rodrigues' study, *Industrialização e Atitudes Operarias* (Brasiliense: São Paulo, 1970), is based on interviews conducted in 1963 with 86 skilled and semiskilled factory workers.
[14]*Ibid.*, p. 108.
[15]*Ibid.*
[16]Landsberger, "The Labor Elite," p. 275.

We conclude that in the competition for leadership, ideologically less extreme elements triumph over more extreme ones, provided they are vigorously progressive. The mass of labor follows extreme ideologies only where no genuinely progressive alternative exists, as in Guatemala, or where previously progressive leaders move toward the center or right or are replaced by individuals of this orientation.[17]

To gauge the degree of radicalism among Chilean labor leaders, Landsberger and Inkeles questioned their respondents on the extent and rapidity of desired structural changes. Less than one per cent of the respondents in both studies favored "total and immediate change."[18] Responses to Rodrigues' question concerning measures to improve the workers' situation placed "structural reform" in fifth position, far behind amelioration of the economic situation, agrarian reform, "good government," and improved educational opportunities.[19]

In the area of labor-management relations, only 9 per cent of all labor leaders in Landsberger's study were convinced that they would be unable to obtain satisfaction of their chief demand in the next round of negotiations with management; 45 per cent were certain that they would and most attributed this expectation to good will on the part of management.[20] Lodge, too, has noted the same lack of hostility toward employers on the part of organized labor as have Landsberger and Inkeles. "Most astonishingly," he remarks, these studies "have revealed that Latin American workers are not generally in the least antagonistic to foreign enterprises." On the contrary, he reports that even labor leaders who were said to be Communists desired more, not fewer, American enterprises, because they are easier to organize and pay the highest

---

[17]*Ibid.*, p. 271. Cf. Lodge, who attributes the *Violencia* in Colombia to a breakdown in the political structure: "Lacking organization and access to power, the Colombian peasantry drifted in a limbo of aimless violence. This might have been avoided if the Colombian peasant organization, FANAL, had had something of the capacity and opportunity of Venezuela's *campesino* federation and the political system some of the characteristics of Venezuela's"; in Lodge, *op. cit.*, p. 272.

[18]Landsberger, "The Labor Elite," p. 276.

[19]Rodrigues, *op. cit.*, p. 134. Louis W. Goodman notes the same phenomenon of union emphasis on bread-and-butter goals to the exclusion of major societal transformation, but attributes it to Latin American labor laws, which contain generous provisions on work conditions, combined with inhibiting restrictions on the formation and functioning of unions, resulting, he claims, in the fragmentation of the work force. These factors, plus the dependence of the workers on the government rather than on the employers for satisfaction of many of their wage and welfare demands, account, in Goodman's view, for the fact that "unions rarely take the lead in battles to transform economic, political, and social structures in Latin America, and concentrate their energies on keeping worker wages ahead of galloping inflation"; in Davis and Goodman, *op. cit.*, pp. 232 and 234.

[20]Landsberger, "The Labor Elite," p. 273. One-fourth of Landsberger's respondents considered that union-management relations were "very good," 48 per cent "more good than bad," 23 per cent "more bad than good," and only 3 per cent "very bad"—i.e., nearly three-fourths of the labor leaders considered union-management relations good or better. Landsberger *et al.*, in Davis and Goodman, p. 241. Goodman points out that Landsberger's data on labor leaders' apparent satisfaction with labor-management relations should be considered in the light of the fact that Landsberger's respondents were leaders of some of the strongest unions in Chile.

wages and benefits.[21] Former Chilean President Salvador Allende himself took cognizance of this attitude of the workers in an interview in 1972: "We know of a poll taken in Chile by a French sociologist who asked the workers if they thought that the big foreign companies help in development, and 78 per cent of them answered that foreign capital is a positive factor."[22]

On the question of worker participation in management decisions, the authors of *Industrialism and Industrial Man* concluded that "serious interest in intensive participation appears to be limited to a minority of the work-force and citizenry, albeit this proportion may show some . . . rise with industrialization." Moreover, they noted, "the careful studies of worker participation that have been made in both Eastern and Western countries do not suggest that any sustained interest in participation at the workplace has compelled drastic changes in workers' organizations."[23]

From his study of post-nationalization Chile, James Petras concluded that worker attitudes toward participation vary considerably among different industries and even within the same industry, and therefore it is difficult to generalize whether workers tend to favor higher salaries (economism) or participation in the firm (workers' control). For example, "the copper workers in Chuquicamata are *salary conscious,* not *class conscious.* . . . Participation in the copper mines is very low, except in some sections of the mines." Among the textile workers, the desire for participation versus satisfaction with more limited economic goals seems to divide along occupational and skill lines: "The main base of support for the notion of workers' participation lies with the trade union activists and the skilled workers; lower management and the unskilled workers are less involved and tend to view the process of change somewhat more in 'economist' terms."[24]

The preoccupation of workers with their own economic welfare goes a long way toward explaining the lack of radicalism of organized labor and the ambivalent attitude toward solidarity of organized urban workers with either their unskilled, unemployed, or agrarian counterparts. In their Brazilian study, Touraine and Pécaut found that in São Paulo, "workers oscillate between defense of their interests as skilled workers . . . and solidarity with the un-

---

[21]Lodge, *op. cit.,* p. 262.

[22]*Chile Hoy,* June 30, 1972. Allende added rhetorically: "Is it, therefore, possible to create an anti-imperialist mentality and educate the people without being aggressive with the imperalists?"

[23]*International Labour Review, op. cit.,* p. 536.

[24]James Petras, "Chile: Nationalization, Socio-Economic Change, and Popular Participation," in Petras, ed., *Latin America: From Dependence to Revolution* (New York: John Wiley & Sons, 1973), pp. 43 and 53. Petras conducted forty open-ended, unstructured interviews in two copper mines, a textile factory, farms, and an urban squatter settlement.

skilled masses.''[25] Landsberger, too, noted the predominance among workers of goals oriented more toward immediate personal gain as opposed to ideological and system-wide goals.

In his study of labor in Peru, Payne also found that labor was basically nonideological and interested chiefly in economic gain, and that this orientation acted as a brake on the more ideological labor leaders. He observed that Peruvian workers resist efforts by politicians to manipulate them for political ends, a frequent occurrence in Latin America where labor unions are often appendages of political parties:

> Whether for good or evil, most Peruvian workers today are self-centered. They resent losing pay through strikes which bring no benefit to them. They also resent, when they are aware of it, being used as tools for a political party.[26]

According to Payne, "opposition party and extremist labor leaders find the rank and file too conservative . . . ." Attempts by such labor leaders to mobilize the workers in support of political causes sometimes backfire:

> The rank and file resistance to opposition and extremist party leaders may be reflected in . . . worker withdrawal from the union, rank and file rejection of leadership at elections, or membership apathy.[27]

On the subject of union intervention in politics, Rodrigues' findings parallel those of Payne and Landsberger. An average of 37 per cent of Rodrigues' subjects felt that unions should intervene in politics, while 58.5 per cent did not (the remaining responses were noncommital).[28]

As these findings reveal, class consciousness among the workers Rodrigues interviewed was only weakly articulated. The absence of militant class consciousness has been attributed to the very social service nature of Brazilian unions that Rodrigues found attracts workers to them initially.[29] Moreover, militating against the formation of a class consciousness is the attitude of resignation manifested by the workers themselves, who fatalistically regard the fundamental dichotomy between rich and poor as a natural and inalterable fact of life, rather than as being determined by the transient phenomenon of control over the means of production. As Rodrigues observed, the workers' rejection of the notion of the special nature of their condition not only renders more difficult the task of integrating them as a class. It also impedes the

---

[25] Alain Touraine and Daniel Pécaut, "Working-Class Consciousness and Economic Development in Latin America," in Irving Louis Horowitz, ed., *Masses in Latin America* (New York: Oxford University Press, 1970), p.76.

[26] Payne, *op. cit.*, p. 262.

[27] *Ibid*, pp. 92-93.

[28] Rodrigues, *op. cit.*, p. 171, Table 49.

[29] Kenneth P. Erickson, Patrick V. Peppe, and Hobert A. Spalding, Jr., "Research on the Working Class and Organized Labor in Argentina, Brazil, and Chile: What is Left to be Done," draft manuscript.

formation of a "worker outlook" and participation in union activities. Therefore, he added, ideological class appeals have little impact on these worker groups.[30]

Thus, to reply to the question posed at the outset of this chapter, the available evidence at this time suggests that Latin American labor is more likely to work for gradual, incremental change than to lend its support to those who advocate violent revolution. Celso Furtado, former Brazilian Minister of Planning, extrapolating from the present actions of both the conventional organized unions and the rural movements, speculated that it is the latter that are more likely to be the precipitators of violent change. The conventional unions, in his view, perceive that they have much to gain, in terms of a genuinely improved standard of living, by working within the system. The landless peasants, conversely, often confronting a rigid, archaic rural structure, may be driven to support violent overthrow of that system. The presence or absence of violence may depend on both the organizations themselves and the responsiveness of the sociopolitical milieu in which they exist.[31]

CHURCH OPTIONS IN THE
LATIN AMERICAN REVOLUTION

We have seen how the Catholic Church at various levels and the Catholic-oriented labor movement have responded to the profound social, economic, and political changes surging through Latin America, by adopting approaches that were characterized as "centrist-reformist," "leftist-reformist," and "extreme left" or "radical." Numerous representatives of the clergy and the Catholic labor movement were cited who believe that existing Latin American institutions no longer meet the requirements of development or social justice, and that the Church must seize the initiative in providing doctrinal orientation and even by taking direct action to accomplish rapid social change. Others, chiefly radical priests (and university students), who believe that the existing system is fundamentally wrong and uncorrectible, demand that Catholics enlist in the ranks of those who are working for the total transformation of the

---

[30]Rodrigues, op. cit., p. 184.
[31]Reported by Wendell C. Gordon, in Davis and Goodman, op. cit. p. 240. An opposing view of the revolutionary nature—or at least potential—of the workers in developing countries, including Latin America, is expressed by Richard Sandbrook in "The Working Class in the Future of the Third World," World Politics, Vol. XXV, No. 3, April 1973. He asserts that since Latin America is "already mostly urban, the peasantry in many cases no longer represents the major social force. Revolutions, to succeed, will increasingly require the active intervention of urban elements, including the working class" (p. 477). He rejects the arguments of those who maintain that the relatively privileged status of urban workers defuses their revolutionary potential, contending that the latter is a function of perception, not objective condition, and he foresees the "confluence of certain [unnamed] factors" that "will radicalize certain labor movements" (pp. 477-78).

system—even if this means working with the Communists. This final section discusses various suggestions that have been advanced as to how the Church might become more relevant to the changed context in which it exists, and particularly more responsive to the attitudes of workers.

Today, although some elements within the Church would clearly prefer to curb the pace of change, the traditional image of the Catholic Church as a bastion of conservatism is no longer valid. In fact, one well-informed commentator has gone so far as to state that "no institution in Latin America is changing more rapidly than the Catholic Church."[32] The significance of this transformation is apparent when one considers, first, the vast influence the Catholic Church potentially commands in a region in which over 90 per cent of the people are at least nominally Catholic. Moreover, as Lodge correctly observed, this transformation is significant because of another characteristic of the Catholic Church in Latin America: it is "one of the very few organizations which can communicate with the poor and at the same time maintain access to power at the top of the structure."[33] Third, the Catholic Church is ideologically perhaps the most innovative force in Latin America. Its approach to the conceptualization of social change as a process of *conscientização,* although open to both moderate interpretations as a technique of education and human development, and radical interpretations as a device for abetting the revolutionary transformation of society, has been called "the major contribution of the Church in the transformation of Latin America."[34] And finally, the Church possesses a wide range of resources for implementing its ideas and policies, not only in terms of money and personnel, but also in terms of communications media and its network of specialized functional organizations.

As an outgrowth of the encouragement of pluralism by Vatican Council II and the emergence of distinctive national Catholic conferences, Latin American Catholicism is turning increasingly to the particular nation-state as the salient arena for its programs and activities. "By incarnating itself within the nation," noted Williams, "the religion is complementing and encouraging nation-building and quite consciously allying itself with the nation-builders."[35] Therefore, he continued, today "Latin America is no longer depicted as a Catholic social order intrinsically receptive to the pleas and programs of the

---

[32]Thomas G. Sanders, "The Church in Latin America," *Foreign Affairs,* January 1970.

[33]Lodge, *op. cit.,* p. 209; Lodge concurs in Sanders' assessment above, stating that the Church "is becoming the most formidable engine of change in Latin America" (p. 188).

[34]Thomas Sanders, "El Papel Cambiante de la Iglesia," *Problemas Internacionales,* January-February 1973, p.8.

[35]Edward J. Williams, "The Emergence of the Secular Nation-State and Latin American Catholicism," *Comparative Politics,* Vol. 5, No. 2. January 1973, p. 269.

Roman religion. . . . Secular pluralism becomes . . . a good to be pursued. . . ."[36] It follows from this new orientation that the Church today is moving in the direction of designing its programs with more limited socioeconomic, rather than sweeping confessional or political, problems in mind. Furthermore, it directs its activities to society at large, rather than to a particular segment, trade union, or party, and accepts or even encourages the autonomy of Catholic lay interest groups. The CELAM meeting in Medellín in 1968 is a kind of benchmark denoting the Church's transition from a body that sought to be the sole arbiter of morality to one that unconditionally recognizes the merits of social and political pluralism.[37] This acceptance of a less ambitious and all-encompassing role for the Church by the bishops at Medellín signifies the renunciation of any pretense of possessing the only answer to Latin America's problems and the readiness to work with other institutions in seeking solutions.

In his comprehensive theoretical discussion of the changing strategies of Catholic Church influence in Latin America, Ivan Vallier describes the priest's primary role as gradually changing from that of "missionary and militant organizer" to "program developer and agent of change" to "pastor and spiritual leader."[38] The Church simultaneously comes to accept a pluralistic participation in society in preference to its previous either defensive motivation or its ambitious attempt to provide a total religious foundation for change. Thus, the Church comes to focus on its pastoral and religious dimension, remaining a part of society as a whole but differentiated from it, and without any direct political ties to either the established regime or to any contending political faction. As the Jesuit Archbishop of Quito, Cardinal Pablo Muñoz Vega, observed: "It is one thing to educate consciences, even about politics, and another thing to get involved in politics. Our action should be above political parties; our task is not a political one."[39]

Thus, as an alternative to the past intense politicization, some observers see an emerging pattern of Church-State interaction characterized by aloofness or detachment from partisan politics. Such a posture would allow the Church to concentrate on its role of "national value-creator, cultural leader, and moral

---

[36]*Ibid*, p. 272.

[37]Thomas Sanders, "El Papel Cambiante de la Iglesia," p. 8; see also Luigi Einaudi *et al.*, *Latin American Institutional Development: The Changing Catholic Church* (Santa Monica, California: The RAND Corporation, 1969), pp. 41-43.

[38]Vallier's five stages of Church-polity relationship—monopoly, political, missionary, social development, and cultural-pastoral—are summarized in Table 4.1 in his book, *Catholicism, Social Control, and Modernization in Latin America* (Englewood Cliffs, N.J.: Prentice Hall, 1970); see also Vallier, "Extraction, Insulation, and Re-entry: Toward a Theory of Religious Change," in Henry A. Landsberger, ed., *The Church and Social Change in Latin America* (Notre Dame, Indiana: University of Notre Dame Press, 1970); and Vallier, "Religious Elites: Differentiations and Developments in Roman Catholicism," in Seymour Martin Lipset and Aldo Solari, *op. cit.*, pp. 190-232.

[39]*La Nación* (San José, Costa Rica), May 12, 1971.

critic" based on application of the Church doctrine of social justice.[40] This concentration on the "prophetic mission" of Latin American Catholicism, within the legitimate realm of the pastoral functions of the Church, would have the additional benefit of healing some of the divisions within the presently fragmented Church, which threaten its religious unity. As the Archbishop of Panama, Mark McGrath, wrote:

> What is the role of the Church in this complicated period of change in Latin America? Certainly, her role is fundamentally religious. It is not for the Church to take upon herself the obligation of creating a new temporal order. If we were to fall into that error, we would fall into a new form of theocracy, and none of us desires that.

However, he continued, the Church—meaning both clergy and laymen—does have a fundamental role to play,

> and unless it does exercise that role the changes which are so drastically needed for the people will be delayed too long, with growing suffering for many and desperation for not a few. . . . It is this desperation which would also launch us into extreme solutions whether to the right or left, with the consequent suppression of human liberty and many other spiritual values essential to authentic and complete human and social progress.[41]

What emerges from this brief discussion is a tentative conclusion that the Church faces serious problems in terms of both maintaining unity in its own ranks and preserving its rapport with the majority of workers as it seeks to adapt to the demands for social change. The question is whether the Church can afford to attempt to outdo the extremist secular political movements in an effort to establish its credentials as an agent of revolutionary change; or whether it should avoid partisanship and broaden its appeal to incorporate and legitimize all reformist and progressive currents, to assist, but not lead, the process of social and political change in Latin America.

---

[40]Williams, *op. cit.*, p. 274.

[41]Mark G. McGrath, "Church Doctrine in Latin America after the Council," in Henry A. Landsberger, ed., *The Church and Social Change in Latin America*, p. 109.

Appendix

Appendix

Church and Labor Documents on the Latin American Revolution

In this Appendix we present some of the pertinent and not generally available documents concerning individuals and movements discussed in the text.

1. OPEN LETTER TO POPE PAUL VI FROM THE LATIN AMERICAN CONFEDERATION OF CHRISTIAN TRADE UNIONS (CLASC), July 18, 1968 (Excerpt)*

We know, Brother Paul, that all the Latin American bishops will gather in Medellín to discuss the role of the Church in the Latin American world of today. We thought, initially, that some laymen concretely engaged in the daily tasks of elevating and developing peoples, who were also members of grass-roots organizations, could participate in this assembly of princes of your Church.

When some labor union leaders asked that representatives of popular organizations of factory and farm workers be invited, your princes of the Church answered that they "did not want elements of conflict in this conference of Medellín." And you know they are right. We are indeed agents of conflict, because for a long time we have represented action beyond words and militant revolutionary obligation beyond verbosity. Because we are the relentless enemies of the *gatopardos* [leopards]—those who talk much about change and revolution but leave everything as before. And you know, Brother Paul, we fear that in your Church there are many *gatopardos* who are taking the place of the old traditionalists and conservatives, who stagger under the weight of their years and their doubts, but only modernize some things without introducing profound and radical changes in spirit and in fact. This type of *gatopardo* is the equivalent, in the secular world, of those who want to modernize capitalist society without changing its content or its results.

Do you know, then, who will participate as laymen in this Church assembly? Technical and professional people, V.I.P.'s, who are most of the time tied either directly or indirectly to the ruling groups, and who have absorbed in the same schools, in the same clubs, in the same universities, the same attitudes and the same reactions as the antipopular oligarchies. We know that among them there will also be persons of good will and of great merit; however, the concept that the majority of your Church has of the elite is disturbing to us because it is a pagan and materialistic concept. The best people, according to many in your Church, are those who have more and not those who are more. And for this reason the poor, the workers, the farmers, working women and . . . youth will not be present. And to think, Brother Paul, that in this assembly of your Church at Medellín it is precisely the advancement of the Latin American people, and above all of the poor, that will be discussed! But this is the same as usual, and nothing has changed in your Church.

---

*From *Iglesia Latinoamericana: ¿Protesta o Profecía?* (Avellaneda, Argentina: Ed. Busqueda, 1969), pp. 88-89, translated by Ondina Felipe.

2. THE PROBLEM OF VIOLENCE IN LATIN AMERICA, Excerpt from the Medellín Conference Documents (1968)*

Violence constitutes one of the gravest problems in Latin America. A decision on which the future of the countries of the continent will depend should not be left to the impulses of emotion and passion. We would be failing in our pastoral duty if we were not to remind the conscience, caught in this dramatic dilemma, of the criteria derived from the Christian doctrine of evangelical love.

No one should be surprised if we forcefully re-affirm our faith in the productiveness of peace. This is our Christian ideal. "Violence is neither Christian nor evangelical." The Christian man is peaceful and not ashamed of it. He is not simply a pacifist, for he can fight, but he prefers peace to war. He knows that "violent changes in structures would be fallacious, ineffectual in themselves and not conforming to the dignity of man, which demands that the necessary changes take place from within, that is to say, through a fitting awakening of conscience, adequate preparation and effective participation of all, which the ignorance and often inhumane conditions of life make it impossible to assure at this time."

As the Christian believes in the productiveness of peace in order to achieve justice, he also believes that justice is a prerequisite for peace. He recognizes that in many instances Latin America finds itself faced with a situation of injustice that can be called institutionalized violence, when, because of a structural deficiency of industry and agriculture, of national and international economy, of cultural and political life, "whole towns lack necessities, live in such dependence as hinders all initiative and responsibility as well as every possibility for cultural promotion and participation in social and political life," thus violating fundamental rights. This situation demands all-embracing, courageous, urgent and profoundly renovating transformations. We should not be surprised therefore, that the "temptation to violence" is surfacing in Latin America. One should not abuse the patience of a people that for years has borne a situation that would not be acceptable to anyone with any degree of awareness of human rights.

Facing a situation which works so seriously against the dignity of man and against peace, we address ourselves, as pastors, to all the members of the Christian community, asking them to assume their responsibility in the promotion of peace in Latin America.

*From the official English edition, Second General Conference of Latin American Bishops, *The Church in the Present-Day Transformation of Latin America in the Light of the Council* (Bogotá: General Secretariat of CELAM, 1970), Vol. II (Conclusions), pp. 77-80 (footnotes omitted), reprinted with permission of the Division for Latin America, United States Catholic Conference, and the General Secretariat of CELAM, Bogotá.

We would like to direct our call, in the first place, to those who have a greater share of wealth, culture and power. We know that there are leaders in Latin America who are sensitive to the needs of the people and try to remedy them. They recognize that the privileged many times join together, and with all the means at their disposal pressure those who govern, thus obstructing necessary changes. In some instances, this pressure takes on drastic proportions which result in the destruction of life and property.

Therefore, we urge them not to take advantage of the pacifist position of the Church in order to oppose, either actively or passively, the profound transformations that are so necessary. If they jealously retain their privileges, and defend them through violence, they are responsible to history for provoking "explosive revolutions of despair." The peaceful future of the countries of Latin America depends to a large extent on their attitude.

Also responsible for injustice are those who remain passive for fear of the sacrifice and personal risk implied by any courageous and effective action. Justice, and therefore peace, conquer by means of a dynamic action of awakening (concientización) and organization of the popular sectors, which are capable of pressing public officials who are often impotent in their social projects without popular support.

We address ourselves, finally, to those who, in the face of injustice and illegitimate resistance to change, put their hopes in violence. With Paul VI we realize that their attitude "frequently finds its ultimate motivation in noble impulses of justice and solidarity." Let us not speak here of empty words which do not imply personal responsibility and which isolate from the fruitful non-violent actions that are immediately possible.

If it is true that revolutionary insurrection can be legitimate in the case of evident and prolonged "tyranny that seriously works against the fundamental rights of man, and which damages the common good of the country," whether it proceeds from one person or from clearly unjust structures, it is also certain that violence or "armed revolution" generally "generates new injustices, introduces new imbalances and causes new disasters; one cannot combat a real evil at the price of a greater evil."

If we consider, then, the totality of the circumstances of our countries, and if we take into account the Christian preference for peace, the enormous difficulty of a civil war, the logic of violence, the atrocities it engenders, the risk of provoking foreign intervention, illegitimate as it may be, the difficulty of building a regime of justice and freedom while participating in a process of violence, we earnestly desire that the dynamism of the awakened and organized community be put to the service of justice and peace.

Finally, we would like to make ours the words of our Holy Father to the newly ordained priests and deacons in Bogotá, when he referred to all the suffering and said to them: "We will be able to understand their afflictions and change them, not into hate and violence, but into the strong and peaceful energy of constructive works."

3. MESSAGE OF THE SIXTH ANNUAL CONGRESS OF THE LATIN AMERICAN WORKERS' CENTRAL (CLAT) Caracas, November 22, 1971*

The society we have today is totally unacceptable to Latin America's workers, its poor, its underprivileged, and in fact the masses of its people. For in such a society there can be neither a personal and collective advancement for our workers, nor a genuine liberation for our peoples. As long as this society continues, the present exploitation, oppression, marginalization, alienation, repression and humiliating discrimination against the popular masses will only be increased by the privileged minority that holds all the levers of power and decision on the political, economic, social and cultural levels.

For the Workers' Movement, the coming struggle will be a calculated, increasing and unrelenting one to win power. Power for the workers. Power for the people. The process of giving power to the organized workers and people is inspired by our irrevocable determination to break with the capitalist society, by our decision not to be absorbed into a capitalist society that we judge wholly unacceptable for the workers and the people.

The present capitalistic structures are an instrument for oppressing the workers. Indeed, Latin America's feudal, capitalistic structures keep man from attaining human stature and are an insult to his dignity. Hunger, poverty, unemployment, lack of housing, illiteracy, improper health conditions—these are chronic evils in our continent. Freedom for labor to organize is a myth in most of our countries. Unjust legislation shackles the Workers' Movement in many of them, and each day we learn that labor leaders are fired, jailed, tortured, and even killed. The corrupting action of governments, parties and business groups seeks to tame the labor movement, to make it serve interests that are not the workers'.

We are irrevocably committed to the working class. Seeing this situation that is an affront to human conscience, we delegates of workers' organizations energetically affirm our determination to carry out a sweeping revolutionary process, to change the structures that oppress Latin America's workers and peoples, and to construct a new society.

We workers accept our responsibility before history, of devising a new society. The Workers' Movement accepts and asserts its responsibility for building a power base, changing the present relations of force and strength,

---

*LADOC, March 1972, from NADOC #238, January 26, 1972.

and devising a new model of society suited to the needs of the Latin American workers and peoples.

A new society where ownership of the means of production will be in the hands of the workers. A society where the economy will be democratically planned, with the active and decisive participation of the workers. A society where the workers will be the agents who develop a new culture. A democratic society where community and State will be the genuine expression of the workers and the people.

A new society based on the guarantee of freedom—philosophical, political and juridical—for individuals and groups, which will permit (1) political pluralism and dissent to exist, to disseminate their views and to seek political power; and (2) a Workers' Movement to be organized, fully independent of the State, of political parties, and of any agencies not voicing the interests of the working class.

This new society that we workers want should be built on values and principles that start from respect for the dignity of the human person, and keep that dignity as the beginning, center and end of all its institutions.

The decisive factors in the revolutionary process are conscientization, unity and solidarity. In every revolutionary process, in every transfer of power to the workers, all the forces of the people's creative genius must be unified if they are to produce a historical alternative that will come from the bottom up, out of the Workers' Movement.

The Workers' Movement must learn to gauge accurately, with a critical political and revolutionary intuition, the domestic and foreign opposition forces that would decoy the workers away from uniting their forces and achieving their historic goals. We feel it our responsibility, therefore, to warn that the imperialisms rely on reactionary minorities and military groups to preserve their dominance and protect their selfish interests, thus criminally frustrating the aspirations of workers and peoples for freedom, democracy, solidarity and complete liberation.

The subtle dangers and ruses used by the imperialist blocs. We decry the empty promises of economic and social improvement via the so-called people's capitalism, which are held out to mislead the workers. Imperialism and the foreign business monopolies make such assurances to lure the workers' organizations into such schemes as co-administration and industrial partnership, which in reality only serve the oligarchy's interests. These are the same interests that many regimes defend while claiming to be progressive, populist and democratic, whereas they are really dictatorships dedicated to promoting technology and the capitalist model of society.

We likewise denounce again, as we have repeatedly done in the past, the various forms and shapes of Panamericanism, which promise spurious integration plans to be accomplished at the level of governments, but which have the obvious purpose of strengthening outside interests and business domination over Latin America.

If the Latin American peoples are to be successfully integrated so they can resist the pressures of the imperialist blocs, and if they are to take the initiative in administering and controlling their social, economic, political and cultural life, then all the forces of the Workers' Movement must be co-ordinated. The Workers' Movement must consciously and responsibly supervise the various institutions and agencies that can further the formation and success of the new Latin American society.

We must take a fresh look at the trade union movement to help it fulfill its historic mission. The Workers' Movement ought to be able to rethink the traditional structure and operation of the trade union movement, because the present situation of the working class necessitates a revamping of union organizations.

It also demands that we expose the interference of the imperialist blocs, which, far from helping trade unionism to take on fresh life, have been making it a mere appendix of political parties for the benefit of the national oligarchies and the capitalist, imperialist blocs.

The Workers' Movement ought to turn its organizational expertise, therefore, toward the masses—slum dwellers, the marginalized poor, working youth and working women, laborers and every forgotten person—so that the trade union organizations, peasant and inner city groups, joined together and committed to the Workers' Movement, will step forth as the real power of the working class and people, conscientizing them, being their presence and political arm within the revolutionary process, for an eventual seizure of power and change of structures and the social system, in the historic endeavor of building the new society.

Solidarity is needed among the peoples of the Third World. We proclaim once again our full solidarity with the workers and peoples of the Third World, who, like those of Latin America, are putting up an undaunted struggle against the imperialist blocs.

We need faith and trust among the working class to meet this challenge. The Workers' Movement must make itself the power, ferment and leading edge of the Latin American social revolution. We reaffirm, therefore, our abiding faith and trust in the reserves of creative, liberating action, of courage, generosity, sacrifice, imaginativeness, responsibility and seriousness, humaneness, yearning for freedom and justice, unity and solidarity, tenacity, class loyalty and revolutionary zeal that are to be found among the poorest, most marginalized, long-suffering and down-trodden masses of the workers and peoples of Latin America.

The Workers' Movement is convinced that these are the extraordinary gifts and reserves that will ultimately make it possible to build the organized power of the workers, to advance along the road of social revolution, and to erect a new society to supply the needs of man — of each single individual and of all men together.

The Latin American Workers' Central (CLAT) eagerly accepts the responsibility of meeting this historic challenge, with the prophetic confidence that "Only the People Save the People."

4. BRAZILIAN MOVEMENT FOR BASIC EDUCATION (MEB) TEXT, VIVER É LUTAR ("To Live is to Struggle"), Excerpt Illustrating *Conscientização**

The people don't know that they are being exploited, the people don't know what their rights and duties are, the rights of the people are not respected and the laws that exist are not being observed; the people ought to know their rights and duties, the people ought to be enlightened, enlightened to change Brazil. The law says all should attend school, the law says it, but there are not schools for all. . . . The time of elections has arrived, the time has come to elect those who are to govern, the list of candidates is chosen, the people should choose their representatives, to choose the representatives of all the people. Do all the people vote? Why don't those who are illiterate vote? What are the elections really like in Brazil? Many voters vote for the candidate of the "boss," many exchange their votes for shoes, clothes, medicine, many exchange their votes for jobs or for money. Can this situation continue? A vote is one's conscience. A vote is one's liberty. One does not sell one's conscience; liberty is not to be purchased so. The farmers feel the necessity of unions; they realize that united they can act; their right to unionize is according to law. Peter and his compatriots want to found a labor union; they realize the problems of their class; the labor union is unifying. It represents power; unity gives power to this labor union. . . . The people constantly say: our currency is worth nothing. Prices rise from one day to another. Who sets the prices of the goods? Why is it that when the salary rises, the famine becomes even worse? Why doesn't the laborer possess the fruits of his labor? Who is gaining from this? The people of Brazil are an exploited people. They are not only exploited by Brazilians; there are many foreigners who exploit the people. How can Brazil be liberated from this situation? Comrades, he who has come as far as this cannot turn backward. We know that we are in the right. We must go forward. God supports our struggle. What must we do? Continue! Continue until change is accomplished!

---

*Rio de Janeiro: MEB, 1963.

5. PRIVATE PROPERTY AND THE NEW SOCIETY IN PERU, A Statement Criticizing the General Law of Industries by the Priestly Movement ONIS (National Office of Social Information)*

The General Law of Industries, just promulgated, has prompted a number of statements about private ownership of the means of production that try to use Catholicism to defend their privileges and prolong the unjust structure of our society.

Private ownership of the means of production is not what defines a human, free and equitable society. According to Christian teaching, economic goods belong to everyone and are for all. Ownership has to be subordinated to higher ends. The common good is more important than the individual good, for only socialization can make possible an authentic personalization. As for the vaunted harmony of capital and labor, it is a red herring. There can be real harmony only between labor and labor, or between man and man. Capital must be an instrument, something belonging to all.

Human work is what creates economic goods and brings about a man's personal fulfillment. Capital, the fruit of work, is the property, not of a few, but of all. In fact, private ownership of capital is what sets capital and labor at loggerheads, places the capitalist above the worker, and allows man to exploit his fellow man. There will be a just social order, the Bible tells us, when no one "builds for another to dwell, or plants for another to eat," when each one "enjoys the work of his own hands" (Is. 65:22). The history of private ownership of the means of production demonstrates the need to limit it—or eliminate it entirely—for the sake of the common good. Social ownership of the means of production is necessary, then, if we want to achieve the goals mentioned above.

We conclude, moreover, that private ownership of the means of production is today so monopolized that it is not only insufficient to create a new man and a new society, but it also flouts the axiom that the means of production are social property.

It has been asserted that the General Law of Industries eliminates private property and puts social property in its place. But that is not so. On the contrary, the law attempts to control private property—precisely in order to spread it. It would control it in two ways: (a) by regulating free enterprise, and (b) by increasing the scope of state ownership so that certain fundamental industries may better serve socioeconomic development. It spreads it through the Industrial Community. Indeed, the reason why such a community exists, as the law itself explains, is to enable individuals to own stock in the Industrial

---

*LADOC, November 1970, from *Expreso* (Lima, Peru), August 17, 1970.

Co-operative. Paradoxically, then, collective ownership within the Industrial Community enables individuals to own private property, which includes, among other things, private ownership of the means of production. This instrumental function of the Industrial Community thus neutralizes the scope of its collective, i.e., social, ownership.

But collective ownership via the Industrial Community (a) is limited by its subordinate position, and (b) will meet further difficulties in operating as long as capitalistic property still enjoys undue prerogatives. (Isn't the excessive delay conceded by the law for business to become 50 per cent socially owned an undue prerogative?) Besides, if there is ever to be genuine social ownership, there should first be an equitable and permanent adjustment of incomes, so as to reduce the inequalities between the widely varying categories of workers grouped together in the law. Otherwise, the existing structure might very well be absolutized, to the disadvantage of those less favored at their present salary.

In résumé, the General Law of Industries does not bring in the day of social ownership of the means of production. Rather it seems to promote a neocapitalistic sort of society in which (a) after a passing nod to social ownership, private ownership is further spread, and (b) efforts are made to speed up industrial development by tightening State controls and enlarging the extent of State ownership in industries.

The kind of new man and new society that we want cannot be patterned on capitalistic models, because the motives underlying any sort of capitalism are private profit and private ownership for profit. The oppressed man will never liberate himself by becoming a capitalist. A new man and a new society will become possible only when work is frankly recognized as the only human source of gain, when capital is subordinated to labor, and the means of production are owned socially.

Energetic action by a government serving above all the interests of the oppressed majorities can be, in Peru, the most effective means for the transition from an alienated society, based on capital and private gain, to an unalienated society, based on work and solidarity. The country has to realize that building the new society calls for a revolutionary change, each of whose successive moves should steer it firmly in the desired direction. We must remember that such a transition, such a change, cannot be achieved without a protracted period of collective sacrifices that may involve suppression of privileges, belt-tightening in consumption, perhaps even a temporary drop in productivity.

All the above loses meaning entirely and becomes wishful thinking unless we have an autonomous popular mobilization and a cultural revolution to support, criticize and quicken the social tranformation. Only thus can we start toward creation of the new man and the new Peruvian society.

6. THE PERUVIAN GENERAL LAW OF INDUSTRIES, Statement of Julio Cruzado, Secretary General of the Central de Trabajadores del Peru (Peruvian Workers' Central—CTP)*

In the manifesto issued by our central office we said that we wanted to express our opinion on what "Union" and "Industrial Community" mean to us. We all know that the Industrial Community gives the worker the right of participation in the profits and in the management of the enterprise. This has been recognized by all the workers in the country. But the union has the task of protecting the interests of the workers and it is an instrument of struggle and conquest, and because of this we want to make it clearly understood that however much community may exist in Peru, our unions will never disappear [applause]. The unions must become the instrument that assists both this communitary interest of the workers and our own union effort, because both offer permanent guarantees for the communitary development of Peru.

And when certain advisers and officers say that where there is a co-operative and communitary system, unions will not exist, I again ask you, "Are we willing to defend our unions even within this new process of Industrial Community?" [voices: "Yes, yes"] This is the answer that we always expected from you, comrades. The union movement is always powerful and has triumphed over even the bloodiest dictatorships in the world. It has always arisen from the ashes with greater strength and renewed vigor. Never has the solid plant of the union movement been uprooted, nor has the enthusiasm of the workers in defending this institution, this instrument of the workers' struggles and victories, for which workers have not hesitated to give their lives.

In this vein, from this platform of authentic workers, I appeal to the government to listen to our criticisms which are loyal and healthy, to this government that said to us, through its most respected representatives, that it needs dialogue. We desire that this process through which Peru is going not be the usual one-day monologue, but that our voice be heard and that we take part in the dialogue, because there is no doubt that the time has come to know the workers' opinion about laws relating to them, laws which must be perfected. . . . Only the acts of God are beyond discussion, but the law

---

*From Julio Cruzado Zavala, *Los Trabajadores y el Problema Nacional* (Lima: CTP, 1971), translated by Ondina Felipe.

made by man is not perfect, and because of this we demand that the workers participate in the perfecting of these laws.

The people and the government, which are listening to us, must understand that we need productive workers without privileges, and we do not want to trade the poverty in which the people now find themselves for another more difficult and bloody poverty which would mean the loss of our freedom. We want a people who work and produce, and when I say "people who work," I mean that there is a military sector and a civilian sector and that both must work and produce, but without privileges. Let us eliminate all privileges [applause].

7. A MESSAGE TO THE PEOPLE OF THE THIRD WORLD BY FIFTEEN BISHOPS (Excerpts)*

Liberty and Political, Economic and Social Systems

The revolutions that advance the rights of men. . . We should not be surprised that revolutions have taken place and still are occurring. Every established power was born, at some more or less distant date, out of a revolution, that is to say, out of a break with a prior system that no longer provided for the common good, and out of the creation of a new order more likely to assure the common good. Not every revolution is necessarily good. Some are mere palace revolts that bring nothing but new oppression of the people. Some bring more evil than good, only causing fresh injustices. Atheism and collectivism, which certain movements pick up as they grow, are serious dangers for humanity.

History has shown, however, that some revolutions were necessary; they soon rid themselves of their transitory anti-religion and produced good fruit. Of none was this more true than of the French Revolution, which led to the proclamation of the Rights of Man. Many nations have had—and indeed still many do have—to undergo these bloody upheavals. What should be the attitude of Christians and of the churches toward this situation? Pope Paul gave us the answer in *The Development of Peoples*.

From the doctrinal point of view, the Church knows that the gospel demands the first, radical revolution: a conversion, a total transformation from sin to grace, from selfishness to love, from pride to humble service. This conversion is to be not only internal and spiritual, it is also meant for the whole man, physical and social as well as spiritual and personal. . . .

*LADOC, July 1970, from *Catholic Mind,* January 1968 (originally published in *Témoignage Chrétien,* July 31, 1967).

The Church does not want to be associated with the imperialism of money. . . And yet, the Church has almost always been tied to the political, social and economic system that, at any given moment, assured the common good and at least a certain social order. On the other hand, the Church can get so bound up with one of these systems that the two seem to be inter-locked. . . .

The moment a system fails to provide for the common good and shows favoritism to a particular few, the Church has the duty not only to denounce the injustice, but also to cut free from that unjust system, seeking to collaborate with some other system more just and likely to meet the necessity of the times. . . .

The Church asserts the social purpose of property . . .Christians and their pastors should learn to see the hand of the Almighty in the events that, periodi-cally, put down the mighty from their seats and exalt the humble, or send away the rich with empty hands and fill the hungry. Today "the world demands, insistently and vigorously, a recognition of human dignity to the fullest extent, and social equality of all classes" (Patriarch Maximos at Vatican II, 10/27/64). Christians and all men of good will can do no other than join such a movement, even if it means giving up their privileges and personal fortunes for the good of human society in a more ample socialization. The Church is by no means the protector of great properties. . . .

Christianity admits that it backs up all who would build a more equitable society. . . Mindful that progress requires certain adaptations, the Church has been tolerating, since a century ago, capitalism with its loans at fixed interest rates and its other practices that are hardly in keeping with the morality of the prophet and the gospel. But the Church can only rejoice as she sees another social systems arising, which is less alien to that morality. It will be the task of Christians of tomorrow, according to the initiative of Pope Paul, to develop, from their original Christian sources, those moral values which are solidarity and fraternity. Christians have the duty to show that "the true socialism is Christianity integrally lived, with a just distribution of property and a basic equality" (Patriarch Maximos at Vatican II, 9/28/65). Rather than shun this, let us welcome it with joy, as a social way of life more in harmony with our times and with the gospels. Thus we can keep people from associating God and religion with those forces of oppression that grind down the workers and the poor—feudalism, capitalism and imperialism. These inhuman systems have led to others that, though promising to free humanity, in reality crush it as they lead to totalitarian collectivism and religious persecution. . . .

With respect for the dignity of man and of his labor. . . The Church salutes with pride and joy a new humanity, in which honor is conferred not on the money accumulated in the hands of a few, but on workers, laborers and farmers.

The poor—especially those among whom a merciful God has placed us as pastors—realize by experience that they must rely on themselves and their own efforts, rather than on the help of the rich. . . . They must regain confidence in themselves, overcome their illiteracy and ignorance, work sedulously to build their own future. . . . They must listen to all, especially their pastors, who can awaken and instruct the conscience of the masses. . . . In a word, the workers and the poor must join forces, for only unity can give strength to the poor to demand and achieve justice.

Those who are exploited must join forces for the defense of justice. . . . Within each nation, workers have the right and the duty to join in real unions in order to demand and protect their rights: a fair salary, paid sick leave, social security, a home, a share in the management of the business. It is not enough that these rights be protected only by high-sounding laws. The laws must be applied, and governments must use their powers in this matter for the good of workers and the poor.

8. MOVEMENT OF CHRISTIANS FOR SOCIALISM MESSAGE TO LATIN AMERICAN CHRISTIANS*

We consider that underdevelopment is only the product of the capitalist system and imperialism. It is capitalism and imperialism that are generating among men and among countries a violent division between the rich and the poor, and between exploiters and the exploited. This domination is demonstrated in the economy, culture, politics, and the military.

Thus we criticize as being insufficient all development solutions that are reformist, capitalist, or neocapitalist that only help maintain and aggravate the state of underdevelopment. In assessing Cuba, we reaffirm our belief that historically socialism is the only solution for our subcontinent to break in a real and united manner the capitalist and imperialist chains of oppression.

U.S. imperialism and its allies, strongly united by their coarse, selfish and criminal interests, are trying to divide, terrorize and set the Latin American countries against each other.

We believe that in Latin America the real and only division is between the oppressed and the oppressors, the exploited and the exploiters and not between Marxists and Christians.

We believe that it is an obligation for Christians to join all honest men, Christians or not, who are struggling for the liberation of our countries.

---

*Issued in Havana, Cuba, and published in *La Tribuna* (Santiago, Chile), March 6, 1972.

We believe that in Latin America the time has come to fight and not to talk. The time has come to move forward and not to be frightened. The time has come when, to validate the struggle and sacrifice, the real honest forces must unite as if they were one single entity to overthrow selfishness and imperialism on our continent. It is the historic duty of Christians to join this struggle on the side of the exploited. Justice and history are on our side.

If reactionary violence is preventing us from constructing a just and egalitarian society, we must respond with revolutionary violence. We are united with all who in our continent are really involved in the struggle for power by the oppressed people of rural areas and of the cities.

We are united with all Latin American revolutionaries of whatever philosophy or religious belief.

We agree with Maj. Fidel Castro that in order to effectuate the alliance between Christians and Marxists not only tactics but strategy must be used.

We promise as Christians to completely devote ourselves to this immense liberation effort. With our brother priest, Camilo Torres, we repeat: "The duty of a Christian is to be a revolutionary. The duty of a revolutionary is to carry out the revolution."

9. PARTICIPATION OF CHRISTIANS IN THE CONSTRUCTION OF SOCIALISM, Manifesto of the Movement of Christians for Socialism*

We are a group of eighty priests who share the living conditions of the working class, and we have just spent a three-day study session together, reflecting on the process that Chile is presently going through as socialism is being built in our country.

The working class still lives in conditions of exploitation, with all its attendant undernourishment, lack of housing, unemployment and virtual exclusion from culture. The cause of this situation is obvious: the capitalistic system, which is produced by the domination of a foreign imperialism and abetted by our own country's ruling classes.

This system, which permits private ownership of the means of production and makes for an increasing inequality in the distribution of wealth, makes the worker a mere cog in the productive system and leads to an irrational use of our economic resources and an excessive flight abroad of our earnings; this in turn causes economic stagnation and thus prevents the country from getting out of its underdevelopment.

Such a situation is no longer bearable. We have been struck by the new hope that the Popular Government's coming to power gave the working

*Press release of April 16, 1971, LADOC, March 1972, from NADOC #204, May 19, 1971.

masses, and the government's resolute steps to construct socialism. The people's intuition was not mistaken.

Indeed socialism, under which society takes over the means of production, opens the door to a new economy that will make possible our country's rapid and independent development, and halt the polarization of society into competing classes. But socialism is more than a new economy; it also generates new values of its own, thus creating a more solidary and fraternal society where the worker feels proud to take on the role that he deserves.

We are totally committed to this process, and we want very much to contribute to its success. The ultimate reason behind our commitment is our faith in Jesus Christ, which grows, renews itself and takes different forms in differing historical circumstances. Being a Christian means being solidary. And being solidary at this juncture in Chile means joining in with this historical project that its people have launched.

As Christians we find no incongruity between Christianity and socialism. Quite the opposite. As the Cardinal of Santiago remarked last November: "In socialism there are more evangelical values than in capitalism." Indeed, socialism offers man hope of being more fulfilled and therefore more evangelical—i.e., more like Jesus Christ, who came to liberate from slavery.

We conclude, then, that the mutual prejudices and mistrust separating Christians and Marxists must be gotten rid of. To the Marxists, we say that true religion is not an opium of the people. On the contrary, it is a liberating stimulus for constantly renewing the world. To Christians, we recall that our God involved Himself in the history of men, and that loving one's neighbor today means, in practice, struggling to make this world resemble as much as possible the future world we are hoping for and are even now building.

We are not unmindful of the immense difficulties and mutual hostilities that arose between us because of events far in the past. Those circumstances no longer make sense today in Chile, though. We still have a long road to travel, but both Marxist and Christian circles already have evolved far enough to be able to combine forces in this historical project that our country has undertaken. This collaboration will be more and more natural as Marxism is more fully accepted as an instrument for understanding and transforming society, and as we Christians purify our faith from all that might keep us from a wholehearted and effective commitment.

We support, therefore, every step toward a social takeover of the means of production: nationalization of the mining resources, socialization of banks and monopolistic industries, the speeding up and widening of the agrarian reform, etc.

We realize that socialism is built only at the cost of much sacrifice, that it calls for a solidary and constructive effort to combat underdevelopment and create a new society. This, naturally, will arouse the stubborn resistance of those who see their privileges taken away. For that reason we must rally the people to this cause. So far, we are sorry to say, this has not been adequately done.

We deem it essential, too, to start toward the formation of a new culture that will be, not merely a reflection of capitalistic interests, but a true expression of the people's values. Only then will the New Man arise, the creator of a really solidary way of life.

We cannot help but observe that significant groups of workers who favor change and even look forward to benefiting from it, nonetheless are not actively joining the process. The unity of all workers, however, whatever their party option, is necessary at this unique opportunity that is offered to our fatherland for getting rid of the present dependent capitalist system and advancing the cause of the working class throughout Latin America.

The dominant groups are prolonging this lack of class consciousness among the workers by propagating hostilities, fear, passivity and even resistance, particularly through the communications media and by their party activity.

Obviously, not everything that is being done is positive. We must emphasize, though, that criticisms of the revolutionary process ought to take place from within it, not from outside it.

At this hour, full of danger and yet also of hope, we priests, like all Christians, must make our modest contribution. That is why we decided to meditate and prepare ourselves during these days of study on "The Participation of Christians in the Construction of Socialism."

10. DECLARATION OF BRAZILIAN BISHOPS ON HUMAN DIGNITY,
Excerpts from Proposals Approved by the XIII General Assembly of the National Conference of the Bishops of Brazil, March 15, 1973.*

The Church must help those people who are most oppressed to achieve their rights as human beings, through social advancement, by means of information, supporting them in every way, encouraging, for instance, the formation of trade unions, cooperatives and other organizations.

The Church must associate the laity in its effort to make known, proclaim and defend Human Rights. . . .

Human rights impose on the Church the grave duty of opening and devoting herself effectively to the classes who are socially, morally, and economically emarginated, giving them objective support in their just demands. . . .

---

*LADOC, unpublished unofficial translation.

The Church must be fully aware of her special responsibilities, and press urgently [not only] for the defense of human rights in theory, but also for their realization, forming a community where she herself can be a sign and a witness of this realization. . . .

In consideration of the fact that among the Human Rights which are less respected are those which appear in the following list, it is proposed that the Church should commit herself to increasing the respect of these rights and enabling a greater number of Brazilians to enjoy the benefits which they guarantee:

Right to instruction, faced with the persistent high percentage of illiterates.
Right to education and to nourishment.
Right to a just wage. . . .
Right to work, and to the human environment in which this can be realised.
Right to freedom and physical integrity, contrasted with excessive repression.
Right to Sunday rest.
Right to take part in politics, which is especially denied to members of the opposition.
Right of association, particularly in the matter of trade union freedom.
Right of expression and information.
Right to defense, which is denied because of the impossibility of *habeas corpus*.
Right to equality.
Right to the possession of land for those who work it.
Right not to be subjected to systematic processes of political and social propaganda, of excessive and indiscriminate commercial publicity.
Right to positive criticism in local situations.
Right to medical and hospital assistance, especially for rural populations. . . .

Considering that social protest is a right of individuals and groups, the Assembly proposes that the Church should undertake the task of assuring that this is exercised subject to the proper conditions, among which are the following:
That this right must be exercised:
In the defense of truth, justice and the common good.
To the extent that it does not become another means of oppression.
In the defense of a just cause.
In the defense of general interests and not of individual ones.
In a way that always makes clear the aim it wishes to achieve.
Only by lawful means.

102

Only after all other means have been tried.

Against organized injustices and against a power of doubtful validity. . . .

Bearing in mind that the right of development implies the requirements of justice listed below, the Assembly proposes that the Church undertake the task of making individuals and countries aware of such demands and that they strive continually towards their fuller realization in practice:

It is a natural right of man to be "something more" and to fulfill himself as a person.

It is a right of man to live in adequate socioeconomic structures, which favor the realization of men as persons and guarantee for them also the necessary "possession of something more."

INDEX

Trade Unions — ICFTU, v, 1, 2
Jesuit Order, 10, 15, 24, 26-28, 64, 66
Julião, Francisco, 4n, 38, 39
Juventud Trabajadora de Mexico — JUTRAM, v, 24
Kerr, Clark, 71
Labor Unions, 71-78
    Goals of, 3, 11, 34, 71-78
    Leaders of, 8, 12, 59, 73ff, 77, 86
    Rural, 1, 3, 4, 9n, 35, 36n, 39, 72, 73, 78
    Urban, 1, 14, 72, 73, 78n
    Weaknesses of, 3, 8, 11, 12, 34, 35, 59
    See also Catholic Labor Movement, individual countries
Lacerda, Carlos, 38
Laín, Domingo, 63
Lamazza, Carmelo G., 46, 47
Landsberger, Henry A., 72-75, 77
Latin American Bishops' Council — CELAM, v, 6n, 31, 39, 41, 45-47, 49, 53, 65, 67
    Medellín Conference, 6, 7, 40, 52, 68, 80, 86-89
Latin American Federation of Priests' Movements, 70
Latin American Institute for Doctrine and Social Studies — ILADES, v, 27-29, 32
Laurita Order, 64, 65
León Schlotter, René de, 66
Liberation, Latin American, 11, 12, 28, 32, 38, 49, 51, 65, 98
    See also Revolution, the Latin American
Liga Guadalupana de Obreros, 23, 24
Lodge, George C., 1, 72, 73, 75, 79
Marighela, Carlos, 69, 70
Maritain, Jacques, 22
Marxism, 5, 6n, 7, 10, 21, 44, 63, 73, 74
    and Christianity, 6n, 10, 11, 29, 30, 33, 48, 63, 98-101
Maryknoll Order, 65, 66
Máspero, Emilio, 11-13, 15, 16, 19, 62
Maurer, Clemente, 64, 65n
McGrath, Mark, 81
Mecham, J. Lloyd, 21, 57
Medellín Conference — *See* Latin American Bishops' Council
Mejía, Vicente, 63
Melo, Antonio, 32, 35, 36
Message to the People of the Third

World, 41, 42, 49, 96-98
Mexico, 5, 22-24
    Clergy in, 23, 32, 70
    Labor in, 2, 3, 8, 21, 22-24
Montenegro, Daniel, 11n
Monzón, Uberfils, 67
Mounier, Emmanuel, 22
Movement for Basic Education — MEB (Brazil), v, 38
Movement of Christians for Socialism (Chile), 10, 11, 29-32, 48, 70, 98-101
Movement of Priests for the People (Mexico), 32, 70
Movement of Priests for the Third World — MPTW, v, 32, 49-59, 70
    Advocacy of socialism, 50
    Support for Peronism, 50, 57-59
    Workers' attitude toward, 54-56
Movement of Unitary Popular Action — MAPU, 29, 48
Muñoz Vega, Pablo, 80
Mutchler, David E., 15, 46
National Office of Social Information — ONIS (Peru), v, 43-45, 47, 70
    Opposition to General Law of Industries, 43-45, 47, 48, 93-95
Nevares, Jaime de, 56
Nuñez, Benjamin, 40, 41
Ochoa, Margaret, 65
Olaya, Noel, 63
ONIS — *See* National Office of Social Information (Peru)
Organización Regional Interamericana de Trabajo — ORIT, v, 1, 14, 15, 41
ORIT — *See* Organización Regional Interamericana de Trabajo
Panama, 2, 24-26
Parteli, Carlos, 67
Paul VI, Pope, 5-7, 18, 19, 33, 41, 86, 88, 96, 97
    Attitude toward socialism, 16
    Condemnation of violence, 7
Payne, James L., 72n, 77
Peasant Leagues, 1, 3, 4, 37, 38, 39, 72, 75n
    See also Labor Unions, rural
Peasants, iii, 3, 4, 7, 9n, 16, 26, 35, 36, 36n, 64, 75n, 78
Perón, Juan, 50, 56-59
Peronism, 49, 50, 57-59
    and Labor, 59
    See also Movement of Priests for the Third World